ALSO BY JOHN NEWHOUSE

Europe Adrift

War and Peace in the Nuclear Age

The Sporty Game

Cold Dawn

U.S. Troops in Europe: Issues, Costs, and Choices

DeGaulle and the Anglo-Saxons

*Collision in Brussels: The Common Market Crisis
of June 30, 1965*

IMPERIAL AMERICA

IMPERIAL AMERICA

The Bush Assault
on the World Order

JOHN NEWHOUSE

ALFRED A. KNOPF   NEW YORK   2003

THIS IS A BORZOI BOOK
PUBLISHED BY ALFRED A. KNOPF

Copyright © 2003 by John Newhouse

All rights reserved under International and Pan-American
Copyright Conventions.
Published in the United States by Alfred A. Knopf, a
division of Random House, Inc., New York, and simultane-
ously in Canada by Random House of Canada Limited,
Toronto. Distributed by Random House, Inc., New York.

Knopf, Borzoi Books, and the colophon are registered
trademarks of Random House, Inc.

ISBN 0-375-41401-0

Manufactured in the United States of America
First Edition

For Symmie

We had fed the heart on fantasies,
The heart's grown brutal from the fare.

—from "The Stare's Nest by My Window"
by W. B. Yeats

Contents

IMPERIAL
AMERICA

CHAPTER 1

Opportunities Lost

Huge opportunities were left in the wake of September 11, 2001. Most of the world was ready and willing to accept American leadership. George W. Bush probably had the largest field of maneuver available to any president since Franklin D. Roosevelt after December 7, 1941. The Bush administration could have generated a cohesive political force of a kind that had not been seen since the Cold War. "We are all Americans," proclaimed the page-one headline in *Le Monde*, the French newspaper, on September 12, a declaration of solidarity from an unlikely source.

In seizing the moment, Bush's people could and should have set about stabilizing the most serious sources of instability—the Middle East, Southwest Asia, and Northeast Asia. In the Middle East, they could have deployed their new leverage to push Israel and the Palestine Liberation Organization into serious negotiations. Quite clearly, Israel's Likud government expected exactly that, especially when on October 2 Bush endorsed the idea of a Palestinian state. Two days later, Prime Minister Ariel Sharon warned Washington not to "try to appease the Arabs at our expense . . . Israel will not be Czechoslovakia." The administration backed off. Regime change on

3

the West Bank became more attractive than taking on the Likud and its allies in Washington.[1]

In the Persian Gulf, the Iranian government cooperated by authorizing American search-and-rescue operations on its soil, the transit of humanitarian assistance, and help in the formation of the new Afghan government. In many Iranian cities, groups gathered to express sympathy for the victims of the attacks on the United States. Both hard-liners and reformers denounced the attacks. At that pivotal moment, Iran's reformist government would have been politically free to extend its reach to America even further. And the combination of improved U.S.-Iranian relations and sensible steps by Washington on the Arab-Israeli front would have further isolated Iraq within the region. But Washington's harsh reaction, notably Bush's "axis of evil" remark in his 2002 State of the Union address, damaged prospects for beginning to repair a bilateral relationship with Iran, a relationship of surpassing strategic importance. By citing Iran as part of an "axis of evil," Bush squandered the goodwill that flowed from 9/11 and provoked an outcry there; Iran's reformist bloc instantly lost the leverage it had drawn from the event.

As for the relentless problem of North Korea, a major breakthrough with the regime of Kim Jong Il had been all but made when Bill Clinton left the White House; an incoming administration could have completed the agreement and perhaps even improved on it. The case for doing so was obvious, with Secretary of State designate Colin Powell having privately called that question a "no brainer."[2] Powell had been speaking only for himself, but with the momentum and aura of urgency later released by 9/11, the case should have been easier to make with an administration whose other senior figures opposed talks with North Korea.

Negotiation was Washington's only plausible option. But apart from wasting twenty-two months debating whether to talk to Pyongyang even once, Bush's people didn't come close to developing an approach to North Korea that Japan, China, and South Korea—the other regional players—could accept.

Taking steps to moderate the dangers from unconventional weapons, a.k.a. weapons of mass destruction (WMD), was another opportunity missed. The Bush administration correctly cited the connection between these weapons and terrorism. And the post-9/11 world was prepared to help. But Bush and his key advisors, by what they did and have failed to do, weakened efforts to discourage and curb the proliferation of the most threatening weapons.

Passive defense based on agreements among and between nations and international bodies is essential to limiting the spread of weapons and accidents, and to discouraging the use of such weapons by one state against another or by terrorist groups. In their disdain for diplomacy in general and arms-control agreements in particular, the administration ignored a major opportunity that existed before and after September 11 to lower the multiple risks from nuclear and other extreme weapons.

A growing chorus of critics within and beyond Europe deplored the thrust of U.S. policy and objected to what it saw as a pronounced unilateralism and indifference to the interests of others. In describing Iraq, Iran, and North Korea as an "axis of evil," Bush took a line that was—is—radically different from that of close American allies, including Britain.

Allies regarded the three countries not as an axis of any kind but as located in regions, notably Northeast Asia and especially Southwest Asia, that harbor the most serious threats to global security. Pakistan, for example, is likely to stand out in the years ahead as the single most dangerous place in today's world; and Iran is the country that could, if circumstances permitted, contribute most to stability in the deeply troubled places that lie just beyond its own frontiers.

The "axis of evil" passage was thought by some to have been drafted as an applause line, designed to melodramatize and inflate a threat that wasn't likely to become real unless Washington insisted on treating it as such. A wider and more plausible view is that the language was inserted at the last minute by the hard-liners around Bush who wanted to see him committed to regime change.

"Regime change" is the administration's mantra. Ask an administration official about how to approach a problem of some complexity with a given country, and the answer, as often as not, will be "regime change."

The issue appears to turn on how bad behavior can be changed. Forcibly replacing regimes is one way. There are the traditional tools, including preventive diplomacy, provisions of international law, arms-control agreements, controls on transfers of technology, and intrusive verification measures. However, the Bush administration seems to feel that bad behavior cannot be altered by traditional methods, only by regime change. Most of its members distrust arms control and dislike written agreements.

Regime change is seldom an answer. Even to consider supplanting a country's regime in the absence of a clear and present danger to American security is dangerously irresponsible. Among other things, it can stiffen the resistance of elements within troubled countries to giving up highly destructive weapons.

Regime change is an attitude, not a policy. The "axis of evil" passage wasn't signaling a new policy toward Iran and North Korea. So far, the Bush team has avoided developing a workable policy toward either country. Instead, it has tried and failed to persuade European governments to discontinue extending credits to Iran, and has tried unavailingly to persuade Russia to deny assistance to Iran's nuclear programs.

Before 9/11, Iraq was judged a problem, not an imminent

threat to the United States or to global stability. Iraq's weapons of mass destruction were intended to intimidate Shia and Kurdish population groups, Iran, and other neighboring states—to allow Saddam to become the dominant regional player. But the problem he posed, although demanding continued vigilance, had been contained and appeared to be still containable. Indeed, Colin Powell, at his first press conference with the president-elect, dismissed Saddam Hussein as a "weak dictator sitting on a failed regime that is not going to be around in a few years time."[3]

The major threats pre-9/11 were posed by Pakistan; Kashmir, the flashpoint to which Pakistan lays claim; the Arab-Israeli conflict; and non-state terrorist organizations. North Korea's leader, Kim Jong Il, was responding to South Korea's "Sunshine Policy" (intended to reconcile the North and the South) and apparently ready to open his country to the world.

In February 2001, shortly after Bush's inauguration, George Tenet, director of Central Intelligence, testified before the Senate Select Intelligence Committee on "worldwide threats to national security." The testimony continues to resonate. Tenet began by citing the threat from terrorism as "real, immediate, and evolving. State-sponsored terrorism," he said, "appears to have declined over the past five years, but transnational groups with decentralized leadership that makes them harder to identify and disrupt are emerging. . . . Osama bin Laden and his global network of lieutenants and associates are the most immediate and serious threat."

But the Bush administration arrived with a different bias, as reflected in a guidance memorandum to embassies conveyed by the State Department early in 2001: "The principal threat today is . . . the use of long-range missiles by rogue states for purposes of terror, coercion, and aggression."[4] National missile defense was established as the centerpiece of Bush's national security policy, even if all or most of the world's other major capitals considered the venture unresponsive to plausible threats and a potential danger to global security.

It was the Arab-Israeli struggle that preoccupied many of these other capitals, notably Europe's; they saw it as a major threat that could only broaden and become more acute. They have always regarded the conflict as political and social, and European hostility at virtually all levels to the government of Ariel Sharon has become a constant. The Bush administration's unconditional support for Sharon was the source of the most intense anti-American sentiment in Western Europe. Moreover, many Europeans were, and are, acutely concerned about their proximity to volatile Islamic societies; immigration was, and is, a hot-button issue throughout most of Europe.

After 9/11, it became clear that few things would be the same, including the singular responsibilities of the United States. Overnight, these became heavier and more focused. Washington was hardly alone in perceiving that to be true. Other capitals also saw then that threats, which were known to be genuine but had been treated as latent dangers or ugly abstractions, were now starkly immediate. And the United States, quite clearly, would have to develop a strategy built around appropriate measures for coping with the frightening array of acts that terrorist groups might set in motion.

In Washington, questions arose: In taking the lead yet again, should America employ familiar remedies based on the joint efforts of like-minded governments, most of them allies? Or should America take on all or most of the burden of attacking a menacing problem at its source, including most of the cost and the political fallout as well as the multiple uncertainties that usually accompany military operations? Taking the first course was not without a down side, starting with the risk that working with partners could encumber the planning and operation of counterterrorist actions with numerous decision points. The Bush administration appeared to favor a mainly unilateral approach.

On September 12, the dawn of this new era, America's European allies offered the United States stout political and moral support by invoking the North Atlantic Treaty's Article V, which provides, in effect, that an attack on one member is an attack on them all. That was an act without precedent in the fifty-two-year history of this alliance, and indeed without precedent in the history of earlier alliances. In taking it, NATO members were equating terrorist attacks with more traditional forms of warfare. However, as the Bush administration had made clear from the start, the alliance was no longer central to America's strategic purposes. It was left to Secretary of Defense Donald Rumsfeld and his deputy, Paul Wolfowitz, to respond to the Article V gesture. Their message was: The alliance would not be needed because "the mission would define the coalition."

Just nine days after the attacks of 9/11, Bush told other governments what he would continue to tell them: "Either you are with us, or you are with the terrorists."5 Gradually, the administration, along with many of its sympathizers in the foreign-policy community, concluded that the new dynamic in world affairs could best be dealt with by force majeure.

Most of the world feels otherwise and would prefer to sustain traditional methods, notably diplomacy. All sides recognize the essential and vital role that the military must play in coping with terrorists and those who harbor them and in undertaking peacekeeping operations. However, other governments also feel that military force and classical diplomacy are complementary tools—sides of a coin. And other capitals may also suspect that a faith-driven White House in charge of an administration engaged in the militarization of American diplomacy is a shaky candidate for a solo role in managing today's novel problems. Also, several of the other countries—starting with Britain, France, Germany, Italy, and Spain—have extended experience in dealing with non-state terrorist organizations.

Disregard for the interests and views of others carries penalties. For example, after September 11, Washington gave the UN a list of groups and individuals suspected of financing terrorists. European governments froze their assets. Several months later, the United States submitted an updated list with new names. This time, most European governments ignored it.[6]

The administration's dismissive approach to other countries, whether friendly or unfriendly, was a problem for traditional allies and for Vladimir Putin, Russia's president. Bush appeared to have adopted a me-only foreign policy reminiscent of Lord Palmerston's England in the mid-nineteenth century. But those who cite Palmerston's dictum—States don't have permanent alliances, only permanent interests—may not understand that advancing one's interests is normally a process of give-and-take, even if the only superpower doesn't have to give as much as, and can take more than, the others. Can a strictly me-first foreign policy accommodate itself to the requirements of a new and very different era?

Putin is among the most exposed of the leaders on whom the White House has relied. He has invested heavily in the American connection, and while relations between America and Russia are fairly good, they still depend on events, especially events affecting strategic stability. Washington's declaratory insistence on having free hands—the assertion of its right to act peremptorily or preemptively, pronounced in late September 2002—could create a rift with Putin, and did create agitation in many capitals.

With this doctrine, Bush was downgrading alliances. America's allies were not consulted. They and other countries worried that the administration might detach the United States from the body of international rules and restraints that developed after World War II. Taken at face value, the doctrine, with its stress on massive military power, justifies preventive war waged without allies and without UN sanction.

Much of nonofficial Washington was surprised and worried. Many Republicans shared the concern of Democrats and the foreign-policy community. According to Bush, deterrence and containment, until now the foundation of U.S. strategy, had lost relevance. Instead, the United States must identify and destroy the terrorist threat "before it reaches our borders," if necessary by acting alone and using preemptive force. America's transcendent role, the document said, lay in making the world "not just safer but better."[7]

This was not a new doctrine. It was cobbled together in the aftermath of the Gulf War by Paul Wolfowitz, the current deputy secretary of defense, and by I. Lewis "Scooter" Libby, who is now Vice President Cheney's chief of staff. Both were strongly encouraged by Cheney, for whom they were working in the Pentagon. In 1992, Colin Powell, then chairman of the Joint Chiefs of Staff, declared that the United States required sufficient power "to deter any challenger from ever dreaming of challenging us on the world stage." However, the newly official doctrine of so-called preemptive defense, as Anatol Lieven, a senior analyst at the Carnegie Endowment, has observed, "takes this a leap further, much further than Powell would wish to go. In principle, it can be used to justify the destruction of any other state even if it seems that that state might in the future be able to challenge the U.S."[8]

In 1992, most of the senior members of the Bush I administration refused to take the broader version seriously. So, in effect, the name of George W. Bush is affixed to a doctrine that was proposed and rejected out of hand during his father's tenure.

Its inherent senselessness was borne in on all parties, including the administration, when in the fall of 2002 North Korea threatened to push ahead with its production of fissile material for nuclear bombs. Since there was—is—no good military option for dealing with North Korea, Washington drew back to an approach based on containment, not strategic preemption. In distinguishing between North Korea and Iraq, Bush noted publicly that his administration was "confronting the threat of outlaw regimes who seek weapons of mass destruction," but that "different circumstances require different strategies, from the pressure of diplomacy to the prospect of force."[9] He seemed to be saying that Iraq was militarily vulnerable and could therefore be attacked, but North Korea wasn't vulnerable and couldn't be attacked. The same can be said of al-Qaeda; it can't be coerced, let alone deterred.

A doctrine of preemption that relied on very high quality intelligence to identify an impending attack well in advance and then head it off would not raise eyebrows. But Bush's doctrine is based instead on prevention and preeminence—that is, taking military power to a level never before seen, one that would so intimidate all parties that no one would consider an attack of any kind against the United States. Threats to U.S. interests would not just be discouraged but precluded. "Full-spectrum dominance" was a term for it in Defense Department circles.

This visionary theory should be seen for what it is—a doctrine of preventive war. Bush himself stated it clearly in a speech at West Point in June 2002: "We must take the battle to the enemy, disrupt his plans, and confront the worst threats before they emerge."[10] "Anticipatory self-defense" is a phrase that Rumsfeld has used.[11] The notion of regime change is the other side of the coin.

In practice, such a doctrine harbors many risks. It exaggerates the role and utility of raw military power. The government could find itself unable to carry out programs in other realms—unable, for example, to cooperate effectively with other governments to combat terrorism. Special forces and smart weapons can help in that battle, but other tools, starting with good intelligence and good police work, are more important.

No matter how capable the performance of the intelligence community, surprises are probably unavoidable. Thus, measuring performance by the standard of prediction is unrealistic and can damage the standing, morale, and performance of intelligence agencies. They are engaged not in winning a war against terrorism but in managing it—restricting the activities and options of hostile forces. The Bush doctrine, if taken seriously, would mean that prediction would become the measure of performance, because a prevention-based strategy would require sustained and timely collection of the kind of intelligence that is rarely available, least of all in a form that connects all the dots. Iraq offers an example; the intelligence, whether flawed or willfully manipulated, was deceptive.

Predictably, some Russian analysts observed that other powers, notably Russia, could also begin dealing with their security problems unilaterally—adopting the " 'green light' model," as one of them put it.[12] More seriously and more ominously, India, too, stated a claim to the model. Two weeks or so after the war in Iraq began, India declared that it reserved the right to launch a preemptive strike against Pakistan just as the United States had done against Iraq. Pro-Pakistani terrorists had just assassinated twenty-four upper-caste Kashmiri Hindus, and persistent cross-border incursions of this kind had put India's leadership under heavy pressure to hit Pakistan hard. The Bush administration's attention lay elsewhere.

Post-9/11, the administration's tight focus on national missile defense shifted abruptly to Afghan terrorism, and less visibly to Iraq. An aggressive approach to both Iraq and Iran was perhaps the most striking reflection of its regime-change fixation, and its unconcern with the interests of other parties. More important, this pointed up what could become the mantra of administration critics: opportunities lost.

Over the past half century or so, most Western governments of whatever political formation have operated within a band running from the center-left to the center-right of the political spectrum. Bush II is the first to have positioned itself on the far right. Ronald Reagan began life in a similar place, but moderate members of his team did manage on many issues to move policy along more or less orthodox lines. With the help of gifted people such as James Baker, his first White House chief of staff, and Michael Deaver, a longtime senior counselor, Reagan managed to build and sustain a broad political base through orthodox means—by imposing just enough moderation on his core political base. And, of course, he had a strong mandate from the electorate.

"Conservative" is the term normally applied to members of the Republican Party's hard right. "Radical" would be far more appropriate. The *Oxford English Dictionary* defines conservatism as "disposed to preserve existing conditions, institutions, etc. And to agree with gradual, rather than abrupt change; (2) cautiously moderate."

Traditional conservatives, whether British or American, liked to travel downstream—with the current; they rarely struggled against it. They felt their way through situations and accommodated to the course of events. They capitalized on opportunities. By and large, they were practical people, reconciled to continued pressure against the status quo and many of their own preferences. They arranged orderly retreats, containing change by adapting to it.

Although George W. Bush campaigned as a "compassionate conservative," he swiftly emerged as an authentic member of his party's dominant wing, located on the hard right. This Bush is in no sense a moderate. But he is a skillful politician and a relentless campaigner, as much of one perhaps as Bill

Clinton, who had defined the state of the art. And he arrived in Washington a convinced unilateralist.

Bush is, as he says, a born-again Christian, although his actual faith-based initiatives are tax cuts and insulating the country from threats, real and imagined. The massive tax cut—his first step—was crafted for good times, but he imposed it on a society in the early stages of recession. And it was all back-loaded with no stimulus. He wanted a big winner, assuming that would create momentum for pushing along other pieces of the agenda. It didn't work.

What worked, of course, was 9/11. Bush's visceral reaction resonated, and he was correctly perceived to be handling it well, taking decisions and not second-guessing himself or those around him. But he is the first president to lead the country into war and propose a tax cut—yet another—in lieu of asking for a sacrifice of some kind. (Three times in the space of a year, the House of Representatives has voted for permanent tax cuts.) And the budgetary cost of the new tax cuts would vastly exceed the cost of both homeland defense and the added military spending that Bush announced in January 2002.

After being inaugurated, Bush could have shown some sensitivity to the muddled outcome of the presidential election and his status as a minority president. Instead, he and his team have behaved as if they had been granted a strong mandate to move the country in a radically different direction. After 9/11, Bush could have revisited the tax cuts and declared that the new situation argued for sacrifice and for investing heavily in homeland defense and other programs designed to contain terrorism. But in January 2003, shortly before having to decide about going to war in Iraq, Bush proposed a new and permanent tax cut via the elimination of taxes on dividends; the cost to the treasury over ten years was estimated at $600 billion. The Urban Institute estimated that 42 percent of the gains would go to the top 1 percent of taxpayers.

Bush's foreign policy corresponds to the world as he sees it. It's a view driven by a moral clarity that pits the forces of good against the forces of evil. This stance bears no relation to that of the senior Bush, but will serve as a template for his son's campaign for a second term, that is, unless events dictate a course correction.

The president is obsessed by what he sees as his father's political mistakes, some of which *were* mistakes, others probably not. For example, Bush is known to believe that his father lost to Bill Clinton in part because he withheld $10 billion in housing credits for Israeli settlements that Prime Minister Yitzhak Shamir had been pressing for. The decision may have cost Bush senior some Jewish votes and financial support, but it did not affect the outcome of the election.

Bush and his advisors, starting with Karl Rove, his grand vizier and political counselor, drew two lessons from the Bush I experience: first, to avoid breaking faith with their political base; second, to keep the administration's focus on security and as far away as possible from the domestic agenda. Before 9/11, shares in the new president were declining. His approval rating had slumped to around 50 percent. Instead of building on the first Republican-controlled Congress and White House since the election of Dwight D. Eisenhower in 1952, the Bush administration managed to lose support for most of its legislative agenda, except for an education bill.

After 9/11, however, Democrats told themselves ruefully that but for the events of that day, they would all have been talking about the size of their majority in the House of Representatives after the 2002 elections, and which of their party's leaders would be elected president in 2004. "Focus on war," Rove counseled Republican candidates in June 2002.

George Bush senior may be best remembered for his preoccupation with foreign affairs, to the exclusion of matters other than his political fortunes. Before him, American presidents from Roosevelt through Reagan had struggled, by and large successfully, to deal with threats to the country's and the world's security while also sustaining and promoting rising standards of living. They understood that success in presidential politics depends on developing winners, or perceived winners, in the two major arenas—domestic affairs and national security. However, Bush senior all but ignored domestic affairs, largely because of his reluctance to ruffle the feathers of the hard right on the issues that seemed to matter most to it. They included the entire social agenda as well as the sanctity of so-called Reaganomics.

It's clear that Karl Rove has anchored Bush junior to his political base. Far less clear is whether Rove accepts a first principle of politics: that elections are normally won in the center of the electorate, not on one of its wings. It may be that Rove and Bush see no need to rally the center by creating winners on the domestic side if the country sees itself, or is made to see itself, as seriously threatened and hence reluctant to change leaders. In a few words Rove's counsel would seem to be, Hold on to your political base and hype the threat from bad people and bad regimes. As 2003 began, an internal White House document listing the "signature issues" for Bush's 2004 campaign surfaced; it began with "war on terrorism (con't)."[13]

One part of a foreign-policy convention carefully observed by Bush I could be described as: Rock no boats unless and until you must. Shun problems abroad that carry political risks at home was the other, more solemn, part of that convention— and another lesson of the Bush I experience that the Rove–Bush II tandem hasn't taken aboard.

His defenders feel that Bush II has rocked only those boats that threaten peace and stability in the post–Cold War era: the intersecting threats of terrorism and weapons of mass destruction. The contention is that other governments, including those in the Middle East, now have a clearer understanding of American power and determination than they did in Clinton's time. His administration is alleged by many of Bush's people to have underestimated the threats that matter. Others say that Clinton's personal problems distracted him and blurred his focus. George W. Bush, they continue, fully understands the threats and is focused on how to deal with them.

Numerous opponents of Bush's policies and his undisguised thinking feel that he and members of his entourage had, at least since 9/11 and possibly before, wanted to wage war, starting with Iraq. For them, opening hostilities there made sense even though Iraq was unconnected to al-Qaeda. It was the easiest hill to climb, a fully accessible target, whereas al-Qaeda was the all-but-inaccessible hidden hand; and the challenge posed by Afghanistan lay in making a state out of bare bones and an intimidating collection of unruly tribes.

In accusing Democrats of caring more about politics than national security, as he did in 2002, Bush incidentally pointed up a double standard that afflicts American political life. Far too often, the press and the political opposition intuitively cut a right-wing administration in Washington a lot more slack than they would a more moderate crowd of either party stripe. Much of the world behaves similarly, especially America's allies in Europe; they regard right-wing administrations in much the same way that schoolboys view the biggest and strongest of their mates. He is fine and an asset to the team, provided he invariably gets his way. It's best to keep him happy. He may not always grasp what is self-evident or what he should know intuitively, and therein lies the challenge. When allied governments disagree with an American administration of moderate hue, whether Republican or Democratic, they usually don't hesitate to argue the point. But when confronted by the hard right, they more often than not duck the challenge and draw back. When asked why, they are likely to say, The train has left the station. There's no point in getting in front of the train. They are intimidated. The Bush administration's ethos—its ritual truculence—may change that.

At home, the freemasonry of the hard right remains very intimidating, its style blending powerful conviction with self-rightousness. It conveys a sense of knowing best where the country's interests lie and refusing to bend on (its) first principles. Its partisans know who they are. Some have a messianic sense of right and wrong. Ends, they think, justify means. They see only black and white, none of the shades of gray that infuse most issues. Americans, too, come in shades of gray but like to see issues portrayed in black and white and in short, clear, declarative sentences. The army of the hard right votes in large numbers in a country where less than half of the eligible electorate votes. In short, it is effective.

Post-9/11, it became more effective. In August 2001, the ratings in a national poll showed Bush and Gore as being as tightly locked together as they had been in November 2000. Each drew 48 percent. But a month after the attacks in New York and Washington, Bush had drawn well ahead, with a 61 percent approval rating. He then set about governing with a lot more stick, enough so to invite talk that he was sharply tilting the balance of power between the White House and Congress. It has since been called the biggest shift of power to the White House in at least a generation.[14]

Several Republican members of both houses of Congress are as intimidated and even worried about their administration as the Democrats. Just two months after 9/11, on November 6, Bush met with the bipartisan leaders of the appropriations committees of both houses, all of whom wanted to add $20 billion of funds for homeland security. The meeting occurred after the fatal anthrax mailings had closed down Congress. The money was to be available on a contingency basis, meaning that Bush would not have had to spend any of it if he saw no reason to do so.[15]

Members in both parties were arguing that agencies including the U.S. Public Health Service, Centers for Disease Control and Prevention, the FBI, and Customs Service needed more money. They also suggested that additional funds were needed to protect several weapons facilities and shipping.

Arriving at the meeting, Bush flatly rejected the request for funds and threatened to veto any move in Congress for additional emergency spending on domestic anti-terrorism connected to the events of 9/11. He then walked away from the meeting, leaving behind a cluster of members who were as surprised as they were angry. "I was flabbergasted and amazed," said Representative David Obey, ranking member of the House Appropriations Committee. "Instead of a serious discussion we got an ultimatum. . . . We had expected this was going to be a working meeting, not a my-way-or-the-highway meeting."[16]

Bush's early efforts to manage homeland security sharpened the concern. Providing adequate funds for so-called first responders was just one example. In signing a supplemental spending bill during the summer of 2002, Bush rejected a provision that would have channeled more money to the first responders. His budget director, Mitchell E. Daniels Jr., impounded funds that Congress had earmarked for that purpose. Then, at a national governors' conference, Bush accused Congress of not providing enough money for first responders. The chairman of the House Appropriations Committee, C. W. Bill Young, a Republican, was angry enough to complain about the comment to Andrew Card, the White House chief of staff. Under pressure, the funds were restored at the eleventh hour.

Resignations for cause dramatize problems as few events can, if only because they occur rarely. Five days before the war in Iraq began, Rand Beers, special assistant to the President for combating terrorism and a consummate, widely respected insider, quit his job. He linked his worries about the administration's approach to terrorism with its plans for Iraq. "The administration wasn't matching its deeds to its words in the war on terrorism," he said. "They're making us less secure, not more secure.

"The difficult long-term issues both at home and abroad have been avoided, neglected or shortchanged and generally underfunded," Beers said. "Within U.S. borders," he added, "homeland security is suffering from 'policy constipation.' Nothing gets done. Fixing an agency management problem doesn't make headlines or produce voter support. So if you're looking at things from a political perspective, it's easier to go to war." The focus on Iraq, he noted, "has robbed domestic security of manpower, brainpower and money, and could breed a new generation of al-Qaeda recruits."[17] Beers had spent thirty-five years in intelligence work and had served three Republican presidents. (On Ronald Reagan's National Security Council staff, he had replaced Oliver North as director for counterterrorism and counternarcotics.) After leaving the White House, he took the remarkable step of becoming a national security advisor to Senator John F. Kerry, a Democratic candidate for president.

Relations with the White House on similar issues hardened Congressional concerns. In October 2002, Bush was granted unprecedented authority from Congress to wage war on Iraq. Yet in the run-up to that vote, the administration refused to declassify additional intelligence assessing the threat from Iraq, thereby limiting what some senators might say in opposing the resolution. "It is troubling to have classified information which contradicts statements made by the administration," said Senator Richard Durbin of Illinois.[18] And the administration's novel doctrine of preemptive/preventive military strikes gives the President unprecedented war-making power, because the trigger for action is intelligence that he is empowered to deny to the public.[19]

. . .

Most incoming presidents take an oddly proprietary view of issues that bear on national security—as if no predecessor had grappled seriously or creatively with them. Bush's views and his behavior diverge more radically from those of his immediate predecessors—his father and Bill Clinton. The national security team that came with him, although very experienced, consisted mainly of people whose assumptions about the world were also very different from their counterparts in the Clinton era and most of those who had served Bush I.

Excepting Powell, Bush's senior aides are seen by their counterparts in other governments as combining arrogance with a stubborn unilateralism. Most of the complaining is directed toward Rumsfeld and Wolfowitz, along with Cheney and members of their respective entourages. They are described as contemptuous of those who dissent or demur.

Although far less outspoken than Rumsfeld, Cheney is the strongest, probably the dominant, member of Bush's national security apparatus. Unlike other vice presidents, excepting Gore, he is not dependent on the President's National Security Council staff, since his own foreign-policy staff is just as strong. And it has an equally pronounced right-wing flavor.

Cheney and Rumsfeld began positioning themselves on the hard right when they served in the House of Representatives, Rumsfeld in the late sixties, Cheney in the seventies and eighties. Then as now, each was judged to be strong and resourceful.

National Security Advisor Condoleezza Rice is an enigmatic figure. Probably more questions were asked about her during the administration's first year or so than about any of the others: What do you make of her? How good is she? Where and how does she fit in with Cheney, Rumsfeld, and Powell? The last question was the easiest and will remain so. She has occasionally supported Powell, but usually votes with his adversaries. Well-informed diplomats have observed little difference between her and the hard-liners; she usually goes with the flow. Bush knows very little about the world, let alone foreign affairs, and is said to be all but devoid of curiosity about what he doesn't know. Both before and after their arrival in the White House, Rice was portrayed as someone who in this area keeps Bush's comfort level reasonably high. That is probably the larger part of her role. For example, she began to support Powell's softer line on Iraq in the run-up to Bush's speech to the United Nations in September 2002 when he agreed to support a Security Council resolution on Iraq.

Rumsfeld's senior staff draws a lot of attention, but some of the better-informed foreign diplomats worry more about Cheney's aides and Cheney himself. Cheney, they think, can do more damage and do it with less fuss and visibility because he is a more controlling figure.

Other diplomats worry more about Rumsfeld. A European ambassador says, "Defense is a black hole. Stuff goes in, nothing comes out. Even signed directives from Condi's office are ignored. We may be told that the administration has taken a decision on something we have an interest in, and there is no follow through from OSD [Office of the Secretary of Defense]. And the whole process has to start over."

Powell and Rumsfeld, Bush's senior ministers, have each at various times demonstrated flair and an ability to move policy along. The similarity ends there. They are otherwise polar opposites. Powell is measured and moderate. Rumsfeld is neither—he occasionally overreaches and stumbles badly.

Powell is a multilateralist, preferring, when possible, to advance policy in cooperation with other governments and international institutions. At times in his career, whether as national security advisor or chairman of the Joint Chiefs of Staff, Powell has shown himself to be a very skillful bureaucrat. He deploys an exceptional knowledge of issues, a sharp intelligence, and much better than average judgment. He is patient and discreet. It may help that he can call upon a natural comic style and has a robust sense of humor. He rarely loses his temper and tends to ignore the comment, much of it abusive, that is circulated by his adversaries in the Defense Department and the White House.

Powell has all the tools and few real weaknesses. He has a national following, his popularity well exceeding that of any other member of the administration, including the President. He is said to be the most popular secretary of state in history. Senator John McCain has called him "the most popular person in America." In another administration, Powell might have been a great secretary of state.

However, not since William Rogers, who served in the first Nixon administration, has a secretary of state been rolled over as often—or as routinely—as Powell. Rogers was not equipped to do the job. Cyrus Vance was routinely undermined by Zbigniew Brzezinski, Carter's national security advisor, although he had more purchase on policy than Powell has had, and in any case ended by resigning for cause. Powell emerged from the internal battles on issues such as climate change and the Middle East peace process an uncomplaining loser. He also lost heavily on Korean issues in the early going. Inevitably, the deep respect and admiration Powell stirred within the State Department has been dimmed by what some professionals there see as his exaggerated sense of duty to an incurious chief executive who has generally sided with the hard right-wingers. By one account, the White House kept Powell off television talk shows at times even after 9/11.[20]

Serious voices have wondered aloud why Powell didn't go to the mat with his adversaries and exploit his political leverage in the interagency battles instead of continuing to play the good soldier. The question "Where have you gone, Colin Powell?" was posed on the cover of *Time* magazine a week before 9/11.

A lead editorial in the *New York Times* in late July 2002 said, "The President needs him more than he needs the President. . . . Mr. Bush will need Mr. Powell's help if he hopes to secure international support for a confrontation with Iraq. . . . If Mr. Powell were on a winning streak, his conciliatory style might look more appealing. The measure of success for secretaries of state is not whether they loyally follow the lead of the president, but whether they guide foreign policy in directions that advance American interests abroad."[21]

For a time, there was talk that resigning his office would be the greatest service that Powell could perform. It's been regarded by some diplomats as a close question. But he believes strongly in hierarchy and in civilian control of government. By staying on Powell would, in theory, remain a reassuring and statesmanlike presence and possibly a brake on some of the administration's extreme tendencies. By resigning, of course, he could dramatize these tendencies and perhaps encourage a stronger and more coherent opposition to them. He would have to be concerned about who might replace him, not to mention the issues that are important to him and that he felt he could influence. Of serious importance to Powell is the State Department itself, and he has done more than any predecessor since George Shultz to shore up its sagging morale and coax from Congress less niggardly funding for it. Powell's fortunes appeared to brighten in January 2003 when Senator Richard Lugar, an admirer and kindred spirit on the key issues, became chairman of the Senate Foreign Relations Committee.

"Colin is mindful of his popularity being greater than the President's, and he feels he does have a veto capacity that can be used to hold in check the administration's worst instincts," says a friend and former colleague. "He thinks he has a voice." Perhaps. However, the record and style of the administration indicate otherwise. On a given issue, Powell may appear to win the first round, outright or on balance. But far more often than not, his adversaries ask the White House for a review, and Powell almost invariably loses the second round. If he wins that round, the review process is likely to continue, and, chances are, he will lose the third or fourth round or however long it takes his adversaries to gain the decision they want. He may win occasionally, but rarely does he win anything that sticks. In setting national security policy, the State Department has become a negligible influence on most issues, ignored by other agencies and serving an administration that has shown little interest in diplomacy. Why, then, shouldn't Powell have resigned at an especially painful moment, if only to protect his reputation and assure a place in history of the kind he seeks?

Resigning might have made sense if he did so for one critically important reason (rather than because he had lost numerous bureaucratic battles that he should have won on the merits). As good a reason as any could have arisen from the Arab-Israeli conflict. Washington was seen universally as a major contributor to the struggle. America's allies also view the strong bias in Israel's favor as creating and sustaining a breeding ground for terrorists, as well as feeding the administration's thirst for regime change in the region.

Further, by their persistent denunciations of Yasir Arafat and insistence on his removal as a precondition to movement to the endgame, Sharon and Bush strengthened him politically, thereby making it more difficult for Palestinians to create new leadership in an orderly fashion. Arafat's approval rating among Palestinians stood at 17 percent until Sharon surrounded his compound in March 2002 and imprisoned him there for thirty-three days. Overnight, Arafat's approval rating shot up to 60 percent, further evidence that Sharon and Arafat have needed each other.

An effort by Bush to relaunch the peace process appeared to get under way in the aftermath of the war in Iraq. But apart from being seen as both unexpected and belated, there was concern that the damage that had been done to Palestine and its people in the meantime was so vast that undoing it might take a very long time, possibly as long as a generation.

Powell is keenly aware of the perception throughout the region and most of the world that Washington shares responsibility with Israel for the plight of the Palestinian people. He knows that the dynamic aroused by this perception, along with the conflict itself, has damaged American interests, along with everyone else's, including Israel's. Israel must be saved from itself. As the Israeli writer Amos Elon says, "Israel has been unable to resolve the painful paradox of increasing military power and steadily decreasing national security."

It will be seen as an irony of history that in 2000 a national poll showed that a majority of Israelis saw the secular-religious divide as the biggest threat to Israel's well-being. Only 20 percent or so of those surveyed regarded the Arab-Israeli conflict as the most serious challenge.[22]

On March 12, 2002, the UN Security Council adopted its first resolution explicitly calling for an Israeli and a Palestinian state "side by side." The United States drafted the resolution.

Meanwhile, Ariel Sharon had sent military forces into cities and refugee camps on the West Bank to seek out terrorists. The occupying force was widely seen as expanding the problem, putting progress toward negotiations out of reach.

On April 4, Bush said, "Enough is enough." And he added, "I ask Israel to halt incursions into Palestinian-controlled areas, and begin the withdrawal from those cities it has recently occupied. . . . Israeli settlement activity in occupied territories must stop. . . . And the occupation must end through withdrawal to secure and recognizable boundaries."[23] Bush announced that he was sending Powell to the Middle East to push for a political settlement. Powell, it seemed, just might make some progress.

On April 6, Bush called Sharon and said Israel must pull its forces out of the West Bank "without delay." And the White House appeared to support Powell's idea of bringing the parties together in a peace conference. On April 8, Powell left on a six-day trip to the region, and General Anthony Zinni, Bush's special envoy for the Middle East, conveyed to Sharon Bush's call for Israel to withdraw at once from Palestinian cities.

On April 9, three days after the call from Bush, Sharon said that Israel would press on with its offensive in the West Bank.

On April 17, Powell returned without the cease-fire he had been seeking and unable to secure a withdrawal of Israeli forces from the West Bank. He apparently was told by his staff that Cheney's and Rumsfeld's offices were planting stories that he was overly sympathetic to Arafat. By this account, Powell had heard from reporters covering his trip that Cheney's office was describing him as being "off the reservation."[24]

Meanwhile, Ari Fleischer, the White House press spokesman, was stressing that Sharon was "a man of peace."[25] On April 18, Powell met with Bush. Shortly before he arrived at the Oval Office, Bush began talking to a group of reporters, and he, too, characterized Sharon as "a man of peace."

According to the *New York Times*, Bush, after saying Powell had created a "path to achieve peace," "appeared to back away from earlier statements that Israel must immediately withdraw from Ramallah and Bethlehem, saying he understood why it was keeping its forces in those two West Bank cities. . . . Powell's return without a cease-fire has bolstered conservatives inside the administration—many surrounding Vice President Dick Cheney and Secretary of Defense Donald Rumsfeld—who warned there was little to be gained from Secretary Powell's trip and that Mr. Sharon should be given wide leeway to deal with terrorist threats."[26]

Powell had been routed, but he had also been granted a plausible reason to go to the mat with Bush and implicitly to remind the President of his lofty standing within the country. That reminder, if accompanied by a tacit threat to resign, might have begun to edge the internal struggle in Powell's favor.

Is Powell capable of adopting the hardball tactics routinely practiced by his adversaries? For them, the stakes were always high and included going to war in Iraq and taking de facto control of the U.S. government's foreign policy. Powell's presence has been a complication. But the stakes are high for him, too. He's been quoted in the London *Sunday Telegraph* as saying, "I won't let the bastards drive me from office."[27] He has worked with them before. In his memoir, *My American Journey* (1995), Powell says that Cheney and Wolfowitz made Bush I's Pentagon policy staff "a refuge of Reagan-era hardliners."[28]

"Colin is playing a long game and choosing his fights," a friend says. Although his strategy has shown few signs of working, Powell may continue to feel that in time his balanced thinking and centrist approach to issues will prevail when the national interest dictates that they must. And he may feel that his experience and the pressure of multiple problems in different parts of the world will at some point push the White House toward the center.

Two weeks after Bush addressed the UN Security Council in September 2002, the Washington Post cleared its throat editorially on the issue of Sharon and his party: "For 18 months Israeli Prime Minister Ariel Sharon responded to Palestinian terrorist attacks by systematically destroying the infrastructure and institutions of the Palestinian Authority, all the while insisting that his intention was to pressure the very forces he targeted into cracking down on the terrorist groups."[29] The pro-Sharon-Netanyahu cohort in the Pentagon has operated, in effect, like an extension of the Likud leadership, and has scared other governments with talk of redrawing the political map of the Middle East and implicitly turning the region into a U.S.-Israeli co-management sphere. Whether this concern was or was not exaggerated, there was little doubt of this group's resolve to displace the State Department as the principal influence over Middle East policy, if not keep State out of it altogether. That would leave the American-Israeli Public Affairs Committee, the potent Israeli lobby known as AIPAC, as the other controlling influence. AIPAC is judged by embassies in Washington as having stoked much of the hostility toward Iran in the Bush administration.

Wolfowitz and Richard Perle, a member of the Defense Policy Board, have maneuvered kindred spirits into several top-tier jobs in OSD and elsewhere. In 1996, Perle and three of his protégés proposed to Binyamin Netanyahu, another kindred spirit, who had just become Israel's prime minister, that he "make a clean break" with the Oslo peace process and its basis—"land for peace"—and insist on Arab recognition of Israel's claim to the biblical land of Israel. They also suggested that Israel should "focus on removing Saddam Hussein from power in Iraq." Besides Perle, the group consisted of Douglas J. Feith, now undersecretary for policy, and David Wurmser, a special assistant to Undersecretary of State John R. Bolton, a conspicuous hard-liner who was imposed on Powell.[30]

According to the widely respected Israeli newspaper *Haaretz*, Sharon told a group of visiting American congressmen in February 2003 that Iran, Libya, and Syria were "irresponsible states which must be disarmed of weapons of mass destruction, and a successful American move in Iraq will make that easier to achieve." On the same day, Bolton, who also met with Sharon, was telling other Israeli officials that America would attack Iraq and that afterward it would be necessary to deal with threats from Syria, Iran, and North Korea.[31]

Powell and Rumsfeld disagree strongly on every major issue. They are as different stylistically and in how they conduct the business of government as they are in their views and opinions. Powell is moderate in style and attitude. Rumsfeld served four terms as a U.S. congressman from Illinois, and his voting record earned a perfect 100 percent rating from right-wing groups.[32]

Powell, a former general, doesn't comment on military matters, whereas Rumsfeld speaks out so often and so unconditionally on foreign policy that he became widely seen as America's public face in the world. Rumsfeld still intrudes heavily on Powell's business, undermining him in various ways; he may, for example, make a misleading pronouncement shortly before Powell is scheduled to address the same issue. For example, in early August 2002, Powell met with a delegation of Palestinian cabinet members in Washington. But two days before the meeting, Rumsfeld delivered a rousing defense of Israel's control over the "so-called occupied territory." He noted that the seizure of the West Bank and Gaza "was the result of a war, which they won."[33] Much less important, Rumsfeld is seen in the upper levels of the State Department as a persistent nuisance. "He is always writing notes to Powell—petty stuff—complaining about this and that," says one State Department official. "It shows us that he is reading stuff that people down the line here wouldn't even bother to read. Rummy is like an old man writing cranky letters to newspapers. Powell pays no attention to it."

The gap between the State and Defense Departments has clearly never been wider, but less obvious is the gap between the Defense Department and the senior ranks of the military services, which is unusually wide. By September 10, 2001, Rumsfeld's overbearing approach had stretched the tolerances of the military services and Congress to the point that Bush was judged ready to fire him. But Rumsfeld's fortunes changed overnight. After September 11, his high-profile role in the campaign against terrorism probably made him politically indispensable. After the war in Iraq—a quicker and easier campaign than many expected—he cast a longer shadow than any secretary of defense since Robert McNamara. The Powell-Rumsfeld conflict is reminiscent of a similar conflict waged in the mid-1970s between Rumsfeld and Henry Kissinger. They could agree on the nature of the threat, but not on what to do about it. Kissinger favored negotiation, a political process aimed at discouraging outright confrontation with the Soviet Union and infusing the relationship with some stability. Rumsfeld viewed negotiation skeptically and favored a heavy emphasis on building up strategic military power.

Powell and Rumsfeld see the threats from terrorism and unconventional weapons (WMD) similarly, but diverge on what to do about them. Rumsfeld would use current threats to leverage increased spending on the kind of military hardware that he regards as essential in meeting threats that might lie ten or fifteen years ahead. Proposals aimed at defusing such threats do not impress him, although he is actually less ideological than the people around him and less so than Cheney.

Rumsfeld is as bold and as relentless as any modern ministerial figure in Washington. Kissinger cited him as the only player who ever beat him bureaucratically. But Rumsfeld didn't just beat Kissinger; he neutered him in a major palace coup that occurred over Halloween weekend in 1975.

Gerald Ford was president then, Nelson Rockefeller vice president. Rumsfeld was Ford's chief of staff, Cheney the deputy chief of staff. Kissinger was both national security advisor and secretary of state. James Schlesinger was secretary of defense. William Colby was director of Central Intelligence.

The "Halloween Massacre" was an amazing set of moves taken by the Ford White House and orchestrated by Rumsfeld. Schlesinger was fired, and Rumsfeld was named to succeed him. Cheney replaced Rumsfeld as chief of staff. Kissinger lost his national security advisor's post and, with it, his direct access to the President. Colby was removed, and George Bush I was instructed to return from the embassy in Beijing to replace him at the CIA. Perhaps most important, Rockefeller was informed that he would not be on the ticket when Ford ran for president the following year.

What lay behind this *pièce de théâtre* was clear only to principals and their senior staff. "Don engineered the massacre," one of them said. "He got Jim fired. He caused Bush to go the CIA and himself to defense. He wanted to turn around the defense budget and be a real tough guy. He dedicated himself to that. He wanted to get his credentials in line."

The people around Ford were hearing the hoofbeats of Ronald Reagan, an anti-arms-control hard-liner who, they feared, might make off with the nomination. Kissinger had been planning a trip to Moscow to wrap up an agreement on limiting strategic nuclear weapons, known as the SALT II treaty. But Rumsfeld had different priorities: he wanted to harden the administration's anti-Soviet line, and replace Rockefeller on the ticket. Failing that, he intended to burnish his government credentials and then run for president himself one day.[34]

Arranging to shift Bush from China to the top CIA job was designed to remove him from contention for the second spot on the ticket. As for SALT II, the treaty was drawing heavy fire from Republican hard-liners, starting with Reagan. Some of them were counting on Rumsfeld to divide Ford from Kissinger and scuttle efforts to get a treaty. In his new role, he did just that. The nearly completed agreement lay lifeless for the balance of Ford's term. " 'He cost you the election,' one of Ford's advisors remembers saying to him. Ford, he said, agreed. 'It was the only time I ever heard him reveal this feeling.' "[35]

In campaigning against Jimmy Carter, the challenger, Ford couldn't lay claim to a winner on either the domestic or the foreign-policy side. But a treaty limiting strategic weapons would have provided some bragging rights and might have turned a very close election in his favor, as many people close to Ford thought it would. Whether it would have had that effect isn't clear. What is clear, though, is that the absence of Rockefeller on the ticket did deny Ford New York's electoral votes, and hence the election. Put differently, Carter owed his election to the aggressive maneuvering of Donald Rumsfeld.

CHAPTER 2

Iraq: A Dubious War

On March 6, 2003, twelve days before the attack on Iraq began, President George W. Bush held a live news conference, only the second such "prime time" event of his tenure. Most of the questions dealt with Iraq, but no one asked about how an invasion would affect the region or bear on the Middle East peace process. Resident foreign diplomats were disgusted, as much with the press as with Bush.

Bush ended the news conference with the comment, "My job is to protect America, and that's exactly what I'm going to do."[1] Four times he linked his intentions to 9/11. But no one asked him to explain the link between Iraq and 9/11, although many of those who were there doubted the existence of one. About three weeks earlier, Robert S. Mueller III, the FBI director, had told a Senate committee, "The al-Qaeda network will remain for the foreseeable future the most immediate and serious threat facing this country. . . . The organization maintains the ability and the intent to inflict significant casualties in the U.S. with little warning."[2]

On the day before Bush's news conference, Russia joined with France and Germany in pledging to block any UN resolution authorizing war in Iraq. This gesture by Putin surprised most of official Washington, where it had been assumed that he would not risk upsetting his alliance with the administration.

Other countries had complained that making war on Iraq, or even gearing up for it, would disrupt the campaign against terrorism, which they regarded as more urgent and the threat it posed as more imminent. They complained as well about the administration's lack of clarity. They asked, What is the United States trying to do? Where is it headed, and maybe taking them? If Iraq is the target, will Iran and/or North Korea be next? If weapons of mass destruction are the problem with these countries, why not adopt a political approach—negotiate some restrictions or agreed limits on the weapons and normalize relations in the process, as the Europeans have done with Iran and are doing with North Korea?

By the early summer of 2002, senior Republicans as well as Democrats were worrying aloud about the administration's plans for Iraq. Most of the people in a position to affect these plans fell into two groups, the first of which was loosely identified with Bush's political advisors. Some of them, including Karl Rove, may have wanted to hear the drums of war so as to keep Americans focused on their security, but without necessarily wanting to go to war. They apparently regarded war with Iraq as a complex political equation that yielded no obvious balance of pluses and minuses.

The dedicated partisans consisted of Dick Cheney, Lewis Libby, Donald Rumsfeld, and Paul Wolfowitz. For them, war with Iraq would, or should, destabilize monarchical and authoritarian regimes in the region and, as Wolfowitz in particular envisaged the operation, clear a path toward democracy. Also, Bush and some among these and other advisors were regarded as strongly favoring war, partly because they wanted to take action against an authentic evildoer who possessed weapons of mass destruction. A fight in North Korea had apparently been ruled out as too destructive. Pakistan, although a haven for terrorists and a much bigger problem than Iraq, was Washington's ally in the war against the Taliban in Afghanistan. Saddam Hussein fit the profile. He had even used WMD, and he was eminently beatable. Also, regime change would dovetail nicely with Bush's prevention/preemption doctrine and could be portrayed, however deceptively, as a legitimate response to 9/11.

In Bush's view of the Middle East, democracy and other virtues lay with Israel and could be contrasted with Arafat's villainy. Bush's heart placed him with Israel, his head with those among his advisors who saw Iraq not just as a soft target but as the first of the regional dominos that would fall in their direction. It was a grand design of sorts. And it pointed Bush toward war.

If we'd gone to Baghdad and got rid of Saddam Hussein— assuming we could have found him—we'd have had to put a lot of forces in and run him to ground someplace. He would not have been easy to capture. Then you've got to put a new government in his place and then you're faced with the question of what kind of government are you going to establish in Iraq? Is it going to be a Kurdish government or a Shia government or a Sunni government? How many forces are you going to have to leave there to keep it propped up, how many casualties are you going to take through the course of this operation?

—Richard Cheney, February 16, 1992[3]

American policy in the Persian Gulf—a decades-old legacy from the British—is simple and straightforward: no regional power can be allowed to control the oil there. Saddam Hussein's seizure of Kuwait in August 1990 posed the unacceptable threat. Most countries saw the choice that he had unwittingly offered as hardly a real choice. His pathology captured the rage and frustration, the dreams and fantasies of the "Arab street," which has a need for heroes. However, he struck officials from other countries as artful but reckless; as keenly attuned to the politics of the Arab world but otherwise unworldly, a poor judge of where the main political currents were headed.

Saddam always showed a fondness for going to the brink and an inability to recognize it when he got there. After seizing Kuwait, he could have changed the government, withdrawn, and then been seen throughout the Gulf as the dominant player. When he went beyond the brink, the world surprised him with its seamless rejection of his action and his claim.

The Bush I administration's reaction to Saddam's coup de main was in many ways as prompt and as tactically masterful as its reaction had been to the collapse of the Berlin Wall nine months earlier. But except for driving Saddam from Kuwait, Bush I never defined his goals and purposes in the affair. These remained buried in uncertainty. If the outcome of the fight was never in doubt, Bush did accept the risk of heavy casualties in the ground war. Victory in just a hundred hours exceeded the highest hopes of the people in charge. But even before the bands stopped playing, doubts and questions arose, some of which are with us still.

What could or should have been done next? Various hardliners, possibly including Bush II, seem to feel that going on to Baghdad—taking control of, and political responsibility for, Iraq itself—would have been the thing to do. But no one in or close to power thought so. The action would have broken apart the coalition on whose support Washington had relied in waging war and smacking Iraq with the toughest set of sanctions within memory; the UN Security Council resolutions under which the administration acted provided only for the liberation of Kuwait, not for changing the regime in Iraq.

Moreover, the United States was not prepared to govern Iraq for an indefinite period or take on the thankless job of keeping its disparate communities from one another's throats. There was no Congressional support or domestic consensus for a wider war and deeper commitment. Securing the necessary support for liberating Kuwait with help from allies had not been easy. In Washington, the feeling on all sides was, We've done our job and we have an election next year to think about.

Also, Washington and various Arab capitals, relying on their intelligence, fully expected to see Saddam collapse within six months of his defeat. But he wasn't enfeebled, not sufficiently. And various senior officials in Washington and London worried at the time that ending the war so abruptly could allow Saddam to reestablish himself militarily. And he did; $4\frac{1}{2}$ divisions of his Republican Guards and 700 Iraqi tanks were allowed to leave Kuwait intact. Moreover, many felt that instead of allowing some obscure general to sign the cease-fire, Saddam should have been humbled by being obliged to sign it himself in full view of the Iraqi people and the world.

The victors shamed themselves, though, by standing around uncertainly as Saddam slaughtered thousands of the insurgents who, encouraged by Washington, had risen up against him. Strangely, and of more lasting importance, the Bush I people failed to connect the military campaign to a post-cease-fire strategy. If they had a political endgame in mind, it never surfaced. They had talked about a regional security structure for the Persian Gulf countries. And upon the victors in the war, there did lay a heavy responsibility—and a unique opportunity— to create just such a structure. The Bush I team nonetheless turned away from what had been its and the world's most important task.

Although a military success, the war left a deposit from which the region's current difficulties emerged and gathered force. First were the sanctions leveled against Iraq, which for the Iraqi people were punitive, enough so to arouse other Arabs. Second was the large American military presence left in Saudi Arabia, which also infuriated a great many of them. Third was the Middle East peace process; it resumed auspiciously after the war and even made possible the Oslo agreement, but gradually lost momentum and stalled. The assassination of Yitzhak Rabin in 1995 was a profound setback, probably the most pivotal event of the long parenthesis of the 1990s. Its ripple effect is still with us.

Bush II and his aides, excepting Powell, took a simple, straightforward approach to Iraq—pressing for a military solution, treating other options dismissively, and minimizing, if not rejecting, the serious reservations about invading held by most countries within the region and by European governments. Moderating the Arab-Israeli conflict and neutralizing al-Qaeda were seen elsewhere as the twin first-priority tasks confronting Washington and like-minded governments. Helping to stabilize Afghanistan was another.

The problem of Iraq had very little to do with terrorism; and what to do about Saddam Hussein's unconventional weapons program was far from clear. There was no shortage of opinion, much of it shrill. Hawkish elements favored combining a massive assault from the air against Saddam's military infrastructure with a (hoped-for) insurrection abetted by U.S. Special Forces. The military services always regarded this approach with well-founded skepticism.

Invading Iraq with a force of appropriate size and preceding the step with a bombing campaign, although it would take longer to develop, was judged a more realistic option, provided Washington first did the following: established convincingly a need to take action against Saddam Hussein's unconventional weapons; obtained an updated Security Council resolution arising from Saddam's unwillingness to allow a serious inspection program; demonstrated its willingness to make the heavy investment in money and time that would be required to rebuild and stabilize Iraq; and showed that a generally acceptable successor regime could be installed. Imparting credibility to this latter assurance would be difficult, since a successor to Saddam that various key parties could live with had not been identified, and improvisation was not likely to meet the test.

Moving against Iraq without first framing the long-term commitment in time and money appeared to make no sense at all. It would have to be an open-ended commitment of the kind the United States made to Japan in 1945. The political hurdles here at home would be higher, and Iraq would be even more of a challenge than Japan because it is a more divided society.

Ridding the region of Saddam, however desirable, was always far less important than eliminating his unconventional weapons programs. Although doing just that has been the administration's declaratory goal, its thrust was directed toward regime change.

The other and strongest reason to take on Saddam in the short term, although not unilaterally, would have turned on his noncompliance with Security Council resolutions taken under chapter VII of the charter; it provides for action against "threats to the peace, breaches of the peace, and acts of aggression." In November 2002, the Security Council declared Iraq "in material breach" of its obligations under earlier UN resolutions, especially regarding failure to cooperate with arms inspectors. Allowing Saddam to defy this injunction would have raised questions about the UN's credibility—about whether its mandates carried any force.

As on most issues large and small, Powell's position on Iraq, although unstated, was far afield from the undisguised hard line of Rumsfeld, Wolfowitz, Cheney, and most others within the administration. As the issue was heating up, a friend and former colleague of Powell's who has his confidence said, "Colin thinks we're obsessed with Iraq. He thought that five or six years ago. He thinks Iraq should not be a major factor in foreign policy. He thinks Saddam is a problem and that we may have to deal with him. But he thinks we have many more urgent problems."

That view was echoed by professionals within the State Department who saw their role as not opposing war with Iraq but doing what they could to limit the political damage that could ensue. Before the shooting starts, they thought, the world should see the Middle East as becoming less volatile and unstable; some mix of active support and acquiescence from countries within the region and in Europe should have emerged. The administration, they said, must have a credible and reassuring answer to the question: What will happen on the day following victory?

Powell and his advisors, according to a page-one article in the *New York Times*, "have decided that they should focus international discussion on how Iraq would be governed after Mr. Hussein—not only in an effort to assure a democracy but as a way to outflank administration hawks and slow the rush to war."[4]

Controlling and stabilizing Iraq in the aftermath of regime change was universally seen as vastly more difficult than removing Saddam. Whether the United States chose to invade Iraq or exercise patience, it appeared likely that he would be separated from power by one means or another, possibly sooner than later. Everything argued for launching a tightly focused effort to identify a successor, or at least a transitional regime that could be acceptable to Iraqis and within the region. Although Europe lacks leadership and coherence, the initiative should have been taken there. With Washington wholly focused on removing Saddam and seemingly blind to other considerations, Britain, France, Germany, and a few others—a coalition of the willing—should have done the tough counterintuitive thing by jointly developing a plan for managing Iraq in the aftermath of externally imposed regime change.

Britain should have taken the lead. The State Department at least would have regarded a sensible, carefully thought-out European initiative as a big assist—especially one on which Britain was out in front and acting as the bridge between America and Europe, which is how London sees its role. In addition, a plan for dealing with post-Saddam Iraq that embodied the thinking and approval of key governments would have had some political heft.

Involving Putin also would have made sense, in part because Russia knows Iraq so well and because he might have had some ideas about who or what could have been a politically viable successor. It's unlikely that he would have proposed a Russian stooge. His interest lay in encouraging the arrival of a credible alternative to Saddam—someone who stood some chance of gaining broad acceptance. Playing that role would have raised Putin's standing within the region and elsewhere.

The notion sounds romantic, given the lack of coherence within the EU and the reluctance of most members to get ahead of Washington. They complain bitterly about Bush's approach to most things, but do little else, and were given reason to start worrying about his intentions toward Iraq in the immediate aftermath of 9/11. At that time, the leaders of various member countries began to raise questions with American counterparts about whether a campaign against Iraq might collide with and weaken the much more urgent and important campaign against terrorism. It would be better, they said repeatedly, to define the endgame in the Middle East and restart the peace process there. They asked the related question about whether Washington had considered an attack as likely to worsen, perhaps dangerously, the already serious instabilities within the region.

In October 2002, the foreign minister of one EU member

country, a man who has had more contact with Bush's people than most non-British Europeans, reported what he was hearing in Washington about Iraq. He said that it had proved impossible from the start to engage members of the administration in any sort of debate or discussion about Iraq. Asked what sort of answers he got to the questions he raised, he said, "I don't get answers. They say, 'You've asked a powerful question.'" He was then asked if he or any other of his EU colleagues at any point considered telling Washington jointly what they thought about removing Saddam forcibly before taking steps to restart the peace process, rebuild Afghanistan, and make more headway in the struggle against al-Qaeda and sibling terrorist groups. He said no, adding dryly that Europe "is better on substance than procedure."

But instead of ritually deferring to American hard-liners, Europeans could do themselves and the United States a service by being explicitly candid with Washington. Instead of telling members of the press "on background" what they think, they need to speak to their American counterparts clearly and often. Candor of this sort, however, exacts a price and can earn them a place in Washington's doghouse.

Gerhard Schroeder was put there in September 2002 when in the middle of federal elections in Germany he announced that his government would not support an American-led invasion of Iraq. Germans, he said, were strongly opposed to any such action. His party trailed in the polls. So he ran against war in Iraq, a position that corresponded to his own views, to the prevailing sentiment in the country, and to the political formation that he led. And he won.

Schroeder had been deeply angered by a speech delivered by Cheney shortly before the German campaign got under way. Cheney's remarks to a Veterans of Foreign Wars convention on August 26 amounted to the most aggressive statement of the administration's intentions toward Iraq that had yet been heard. Saddam, he said, would "fairly soon" have nuclear weapons, and would then "seek domination of the entire Middle East, take control of a great portion of the world's energy supplies, directly threaten America's friends throughout the region and subject the United States or any other nation to nuclear blackmail."[5]

The ripple effect of Cheney's speech is worth examining. Its impact on the White House itself may have been heavy. For whatever reason, Cheney's staff did not clear his remarks with Bush's people, at least not in time for them to vet the draft put before them. Regarding inspections, the speech was dismissive, although by this point Bush was known to have been seriously considering a speech to the UN that would open the door to renewed inspections of Iraq's weapons.

Just one week after the speech, Powell broke a recent silence on the Iraq issue by saying that as a "first step," UN weapons inspectors must return to Iraq, and the world must be provided evidence of the threat posed by Saddam Hussein before any action was taken.[6]

The Cheney speech went down very badly in Europe. Schroeder regarded it as a signal from Bush that he was breaking a commitment to consult prior to attacking Iraq. The speech probably caused him to feel justified in separating himself from Washington on the issue.

Washington accused Schroeder of pandering to opinion in order to win the election. Here again is where the double standard applies. Schroeder had unhesitatingly taken political risks by committing German forces in support of military operations against the Taliban. These troops became the second-largest support group in Afghanistan, and were later expanded. Moreover, just eight weeks after 9/11, Schroeder took a major risk by submitting his anti-terrorism policy to a parliamentary vote of confidence in his government. With 666 members, he needed an absolute majority of 334 to prevail. He won with 336 votes, a margin of just 2.

In dislodging Saddam Hussein, Bush is widely thought

to have acted as he did, at least in part, for domestic political purposes. The case against Saddam was an easy one to make, and removing him from the scene was always a more attractive and simpler task than, say, battling the forces of terrorism or taking on Israel's Likud. But Schroeder, by assigning a higher priority to stabilizing Afghanistan and fighting al-Qaeda than to dislodging Saddam Hussein, was taking a position that reflected the thinking not just of Germany but also its EU partners, excepting official London.

The domestic differences over what to do about Iraq grew wider over the spring and summer of 2002. An attack on Iraq would clearly not be a rerun of Desert Storm. Allies, it appeared, would be few and far between, especially in the region. The heavy commitment in resources and time that a war with Iraq would entail strongly reinforced that concern. The drumbeat of tough administration rhetoric created serious concerns that crossed party lines.

The Republican party began to split on foreign policy in the middle of the twentieth century. The fault line occasionally breaks to the surface, as often as not on arms-control issues. It did so again over Iraq, during the record heat wave in August 2002. This time, the open revolt of the so-called establishment wing drew support from a few hard-liners and some authentic conservatives, including Jack Kemp, a former vice presidential candidate.

On August 4, General Brent Scowcroft, warned on CBS television that an invasion "could turn the whole region into a cauldron and, thus, destroy the war on terrorism." Scowcroft's willingness to discuss Iraq publicly had come as a surprise, if only because he normally refuses invitations from television interview shows to talk about issues on which his views may set him apart from the son of the president whom he served as national security advisor and to whom he remains close. But just eleven days after initially going public, Scowcroft did so again, this time more tellingly because he made the case against an invasion in print—in an op-ed piece in the *Wall Street Journal*.

It was an event. A universally respected figure who serves as chairman of the President's Foreign Intelligence Advisory Board seemed bent on demolishing the standard arguments of the warhawks. "There is scant evidence," he said, "to tie Saddam to terrorist organizations, and even less to the Sept. 11 attacks. Indeed, Saddam's goals have little in common with the terrorists who threaten us, and there is little incentive for him to make common cause with them."[7]

Still, shortly after the article appeared, Donald Rumsfeld declared that members of the al-Qaeda network were operating in Iraq. He said the same thing a few days later, despite the availability of sensitive intelligence pointing in the other direction. For example, two reports—one from the CIA, the other from the National Security Agency—reported the absence of any information connecting Iraq and terrorist groups. Rumsfeld must have seen this material, which was cleared by the deputy leadership of both agencies. In late September, Minnesota's Senator Mark Dayton asked Rumsfeld, "What is compelling us to now make a precipitous decision and take precipitous actions?" "What's different? What's different? What's different is 3,000 people were killed," responded Rumsfeld, adding, "I suggest that any who insist on perfect evidence are back in the 20th century and still thinking in pre-9/11 terms."[8] But Scowcroft's op-ed piece had warned that "an attack on Iraq at this time would seriously jeopardize, if not destroy, the global counter-terrorist campaign we have undertaken."[9]

The prevailing views of the senior military ranks were aligned with those of the State Department. Also, deeply skeptical and negative comments about invading Iraq were made openly or sotto voce by various retired military figures. One sharply dissenting military opinion was that of retired Marine Corps General Anthony C. Zinni, then a senior advisor to Powell and former chief of the U.S. Central Command. Just after the Scowcroft article appeared, Zinni argued in a speech that the United States would be wiser to negotiate peace between Israelis and Palestinians, encourage reform in Iran, and pursue the al-Qaeda network before going after Saddam Hussein. "It's pretty interesting that all the generals see it the same way," Zinni said, "and all the others who have never fired a shot and are hot to go to war see it another way."[10]

A few days before, similar op-ed pieces by Kissinger had appeared in both the *Washington Post* and the *Chicago Tribune*. The articles were complicated and, as usual, offered comfort to elements on either side of the issue. One very short passage drew attention by connecting Iraq to India and Pakistan: "The most interesting and potentially fateful reaction [to war in Iraq] might well be that of India, which would be tempted to apply the new principle of preemption to Pakistan."[11] According to some foreign diplomats, no one in government, including Powell's State Department, had argued the connection, even though the ongoing confrontation between India and Pakistan had brought the parties close to war twice in the space of a year. "We haven't seen any cross-issue planning," said one senior European diplomat.

Among those who did make the connection was Republican Senator Chuck Hagel of Nebraska, who expressed concern that "Mr. Bush's policy of pre-emptive strikes at governments armed with weapons of mass destruction could induce India to attack Pakistan and could create the political cover for Israel to expel Palestinians from the West Bank and Gaza." Hagel, a Vietnam War hero and among the first to question Bush's position on Iraq, declared on August 16 that the CIA had "absolutely no evidence" that Iraq possesses or will soon possess nuclear weapons."[12]

On the same day, Lawrence S. Eagleburger, who served Bush senior for a time as secretary of state, joined the chorus of Republican skeptics who saw no need to move against Saddam anytime soon. Like several members of both parties, they appeared to agree with Scowcroft that Washington should focus first on the campaign against terrorism and on calming the battle between Israel and the Palestinians.

All sides were concerned with the political aftermath. There was no "day after Saddam" strategy, according to foreign diplomats. "That whole area is undeveloped," said a well-informed European diplomat in the fall of 2002. The administration had shown itself better equipped and more inclined to overthrow states than to rebuild and stabilize broken societies. Iraqi opposition groups were not seen as capable of organizing a workable or viable government. Nor could a U.S. puppet regime succeed in Iraq's highly nationalistic society. "Suppose we win, which we will, what do we do then?" is a question that bemused people were asking. Another was "Why exactly are we doing this?"

About six weeks or so before the war started, the Senate Committee on Foreign Relations held hearings on plans for a post-Saddam Iraq. The administration witnesses were at a serious disadvantage, since they had little that was specific or convincing to say about the nature, scope, cost, and duration of the occupation. They were followed by outside experts, including General Zinni, who deplored the absence of a "counterpart" to the military strategy. Senator Hagel spoke angrily of the dangers of a largely ad hoc policy once war starts and American forces are in harm's way. "If you're having a problem now," he told the administration witnesses, "what the hell do you think you're going to do when you get in there?"[13] As events would show, the administration wasn't listening; whatever preparations were made lacked focus, coherence, and perspective. The flawed planning didn't draw on the recent experience with such operations in Bosnia and Kosovo. There appeared to be no design for providing security and public services.

Another Iraqi general—a "Saddam lite"—was seen by some Iraq watchers as being the best, or least bad, political answer. Talk within the administration about bringing democracy to the entire region was just talk, although seriously meant. The notion of a one-size-fits-all political system, least of all parliamentary democracy, struck people who knew this region as fanciful. Some of Bush's people believed that an attack against Iraq would set off a contagion of democracy that would sweep through the region. They seemed not to consider that religious fundamentalism cannot be re-engineered—or that a contagion of something new might benefit extremist elements, sweeping them into power.

There was talk that once the oil fields were fully operating, Iraq's new government would be able to function normally. That's unlikely. Whoever controls the oil controls Iraq. It will take time before a "Saddam lite," or any new crowd, gains the confidence of Washington and other interested capitals, notably Moscow and Paris.

Experienced observers of the region were all but certain that the military occupation force that would take over post-Saddam Iraq would have to remain for several years, possibly as many as ten to fifteen. Even with full support from the international community, the occupation of Japan lasted seven years, ten in Germany. In Iraq, the occupation force would have to keep the peace and supervise the program of putting back together a country riven by sectarian and ethnic differences.

The force, it appeared, might have to be largely, if not predominantly, American in its composition, a prospect from which the U.S. military shrank. A prolonged American military occupation of an Arab country, it knew, would be full of deadly risks. The benign presence of 5,000 American troops on Saudi soil was one of Osama bin Laden's more exploitable grievances.[14]

Foreign diplomats worried aloud about the reaction within the region. The administration had done little, if any, analysis of and planning for what various countries might do after the conflict. Would Iran, for example, take advantage of Iraq's enfeebled state to throw its weight around? Or would it remain content to peddle influence with Iraq's Shia population? And what lesson would countries within this region and others draw from the conflict? The lesson of the Gulf War was that battles were won with modern, high-performance weapons, the smarter the better. The lesson, it seemed, of a second Iraq war might very well be that today's armies should have not just better munitions but the far more destructive unconventional weapons as well.

Bush's forceful speech to the UN on September 12, 2002, went down very well, enough so to transform the terms of the debate. Gone were the serious and telling objections to invading Iraq, lost in the cascade of hurrahs and sighs of relief that followed his declared willingness to align policy with a Security Council resolution. Multilateralism was pronounced alive and well.

The White House wisely avoided using the speech to establish an actual link between Iraq and terrorism or to inflate the threat from Iraq's weapons of mass destruction, because there was no such link and because Saddam's WMD arsenal, notably his capacity for delivering lethal weapons beyond the battlefield, was considerably less than modest. As for nuclear weapons, he wasn't close. Over the past ten years or so, he, or some of the people under his control, might have tried to make off with some loose fissile material in Russia; there has been enough of it lying around. But if they did try, they didn't succeed.

Bush's speech was portrayed as a victory for Powell, and it began to be said that he had become secretary of state in fact as well as in name. The speech had gone through twenty-three drafts, not one of which had mentioned a UN resolution. In the days preceding delivery on the twelfth, Powell battled Rumsfeld and especially Cheney over whether language favoring a resolution would be in the text. According to one account of the affair that is directly traceable to Powell, Bush ordered an insertion that said he would work with the Security Council for the necessary resolutions; it was added to the final draft, number 24. However, the language did not find its way into the copy that was put into the TelePrompTer. So Bush, when he reached that point in the text, ad-libbed the missing line.[15]

Powell got a strong assist from Tony Blair, who arrived at Camp David on September 7, five days before the speech. (The Joint Chiefs and CIA Director George Tenet also supported Powell.) He and Bush met at 3:45 and talked until Blair left at 7:45 to fly to Edinburgh. Bush had by then decided to take the issue of Iraq to the UN, but Blair needed confirmation of that and to find out exactly what the decision actually meant. They agreed that war was likely, that the UN would be challenged to find the evidence, and that Saddam in turn would surely conceal it. But they also agreed that the UN process had to be exhausted. Blair needed that sort of cover. (In the end, however, that process was not exhausted.)

There arose the issue of whether more than one resolution would be required, but the discussion was left vague and undecided. Blair was described as "agnostic," according to one participant, while Cheney, probably speaking for most of his colleagues, was very hostile to the idea of a second resolution.

The meeting occurred partly because Blair wanted to link making progress on the Palestine problem with forcible regime change in Iraq. Like Powell, he felt strongly that the start of a process to settle the Arab-Israeli quarrel should come first, and he said as much to Bush. But he did not make this sensible view a precondition of his support for the war. Not doing so then or not long afterward was a historic mistake—in part because Blair ran a serious risk of sacrificing himself to Bush's war and becoming a tragic figure. Most of Britain was opposed to war, as was the larger part of the parliamentary Labour party, including some members of the cabinet. But the opposition in Britain would have been less had the war been part of an effort already under way to bring peace to the Middle East. Failing to do that first, the foreign office worried, might trigger a major upheaval in the Arab world.

Still, of the various players in this drama, the only one who, besides staying on the course he set for himself, acted out of conviction was Blair. In doing so, he also assumed larger political risks than any of the others.

Colin Powell, too, could have made a historic difference. Like Blair, he deplored the prospect of launching the war without first applying pressure on Israel to start a process leading toward the political endgame in Palestine. The meeting at Camp David was as good a time as any to have linked these issues. Powell could have made doing just that a condition for his continued support of Bush's war policy and, indeed, for his willingness to remain in the job he holds.

Had any such step coincided with a similarly bold move by Blair, would Bush, the stubborn unilateralist, have acquiesced? Possibly. Powell had leverage, but probably not enough to make a difference. As some insiders believed, he may have made a deal, probably tacit, with the boss. In return for Bush's willingness to take the issue to the UN, Powell would go the distance with him on the war.

At the Camp David meeting, Bush replied to Blair's entreaty by noting his intention to move toward a Palestinian state. However, a British official who was there recalled Bush discussing the chance of a Palestinian state in 2005 (after the U.S. presidential elections) and saying, " 'I agree with you, Tony, but Arafat is a shit and you can't work with him.'

"We had been successful in getting Iraq onto this UN track," said this official. "But we've failed miserably on this other front. Israel desperately undermines the case for whacking Iraq. We are feeding the beast." He meant terrorist groups. Blair had not allowed his genuine determination to right wrongs push him into open confrontation with Bush on the issue of Israel.

For some time, diplomats and officials of other governments had complained that all the administration's creative energy and its attention to other issues—Palestine, the prospect of war between India and Pakistan, the possibility of ungovernable instabilities in the Korean peninsula—were being sucked into its planning for Iraq.

Powell's notable achievement was prevailing over colleagues who opposed asking the UN for authority to wage war in Iraq. He had to have recognized that if the administration overrode or was seen to abuse that authority, his achievement would look very different. His critics were sure to say that going to the UN complicated the President's life and wasted a lot of time. If Powell believed that protecting the UN's role in this matter was important and/or he believed in the self-evidently vital importance of linking progress in Palestine to making war on Iraq, he should have done everything he could to make that happen. The ripple effect of the gesture would have been very wide as well as very useful.

The nature and timing of a Security Council resolution abruptly became the focus of discussion. Bush's aides pushed for a resolution that set the bar much higher than in the past—too high, it seemed for a time, for France and Russia. The hope in most capitals was that the administration would agree eventually to a version that, although tougher than its predecessors, wouldn't overcome the tolerances of key players. Advocates of a softer approach argued that the United States would need allies not just before a fight with Iraq but even more so afterward. A distinctly multilateral approach by Washington would make it difficult for European governments to avoid helping out, financially and in other ways, after Saddam was gone.

France's proposal drew considerable support, and required Iraq to accept the "any time, any place" approach to inspections. If Saddam didn't cooperate or failed to disarm, a second resolution could and probably would have led to war. European capitals wanted the stress on just disarming Iraq, but many of them worried that talk in Washington of regime change and a new national security strategy reflected an intention to reorder the world on American terms.

As they had on September 12, Powell and Blair prevailed, but only after two months of tough and laborious negotiations. A resolution on Iraq of the sort that the French had struggled for and they had supported was adopted on November 8, 2002. In a well-informed and measured column appearing that day, Philip Stephens, the editor of the *Financial Times*, captured the meaning of what had gone on. "As much as it [Bush's administration] remains unilateralist in principle," he wrote, "it remains, for the time being at least, multilateralist in practice. . . . [The administration] has broken its own cardinal rule by allowing the shape of the international coalition to determine the mission rather than the mission to determine the coalition. As late as Monday of this week, Mr. Cheney had been arguing at a White House meeting that Colin Powell's draft resolution conceded too much to multilateralism. But the Secretary of State, who only a few months ago seemed marginalized, won the argument."[16] In the end, of course, Bush went to war on his original timetable, the mission determining the coalition.

The unanimity of the Security Council in approving the resolution was a surprise. But more interesting was the appearance—illusion, actually—of so many winners, including each of the council's five permanent members. Although Bush was seen, at least at home, as the big winner, President Jacques Chirac did every bit as well from a European perspective. First, he went to the mat with Bush, arguing against the White House version that would have granted the United States authority to use preemptive force. He even threatened to veto the proposal, and he convinced first his own people and then the Americans that he would have done exactly that.

There remained differences over some of the language in the two-stage version, but each side ended up getting what it needed. The United States was left free to attack Iraq without Security Council authorization, but the two-stage process that France pressed for did allow the council to assess the seriousness of any violation by Iraq and to consider how to respond. Also, if Iraq showed signs of having breached its obligations, it would be UN inspectors who would determine whether there actually had been a violation. France was left in a position to align itself with the United States in the event of war, yet seen elsewhere as having succeeded in restraining a willful crowd in Washington.[17]

Neither in the White House nor in the Élysée Palace was there any crowing—no inspired leaks to the press aimed at showing one side as having gotten the upper hand. Colin Powell was the clear winner of Washington's feral interagency struggle. As a strong advocate of the French approach, Putin, too, was a winner. And so was Jiang Zemin, who in his last hurrah after thirteen years as China's party chief not only supported the resolution but took other steps to bring China closer to the United States. Shortly before the vote, China adopted seemingly tight regulations on dual-use missile technology exports, and began discussing cooperation with the United States on North Korea's weapons programs.[18]

Powell's ally, Tony Blair, was the essential offstage presence;

his influence on the outcome can't be measured but, as noted above, was probably more central to what happened than even Powell's or, for that matter, Chirac's. However, Blair was also the victim of the diplomatic train wreck that lay just ahead. Resolution 1441, as crafted, was a spongy document that each of the contesting parties was going to interpret freely.

For a brief time, it appeared that another winner was the United Nations. In Washington, a distinctly minority view had always held that war could be averted. After Bush's speech, this view very gradually gathered strength. The balance between war and something well short of that seemed to have shifted, if slightly, away from war.

For many months, Bush had been the focus of a play within the play. In building up pressure for regime change in Iraq, the hawks labored to leave him with no alternative to invasion. Arguments put forward by advocates of restraint, although strongly felt, were also designed to lower the temperature and give Bush a lot to think about and plenty of time to do it. However, Rumsfeld and Cheney and their cohorts knew they were pushing on an open door. Bush senior had likened Saddam to Hitler, a pronouncement that Bush junior probably took aboard. A bust of Churchill occupies a place in his office. And regarding Saddam, he probably saw himself at times as a Churchill beset by soft-liners and appeasers, as a leader who would follow where the moral clarity led, although not one who would echo Churchill's call for self-sacrifice on the home front.

A moral clarity was apparent in the days immediately following 9/11, but was then lost beneath the wave of hyperbole and misrepresentation to which many contributed, and not just the Bush people. Democrats, by and large, were intimidated, reluctant to take on a president who had with some skill made national security the consuming issue and who didn't hesitate to accuse his critics of caring less about that than about politics. However, among the citations for egregiously silly behavior by Democrats, one might go to former Vice President Al Gore, who stuck his foot in his mouth after attacking the President; Gore warned that military action to dislodge Saddam Hussein would "severely damage" the overall war on terrorism and "weaken" U.S. leadership in the world. Gore also challenged the administration's new doctrine of preemption.[19]

The speech rallied many Democrats, but not for long. Later in his speech, Gore said, "Back in 1991, I was one of a handful of Democrats in the United States to vote in favor of the resolution endorsing the Persian Gulf War. And I felt betrayed by the first Bush administration's hasty departure from the battlefield."[20]

Gore's critics, including the *Washington Times* and the Fox News Channel, lost no time in recalling a very different sentiment expressed by Gore in remarks to the Senate on April 18, 1991: "I want to state this clearly. President Bush should not be blamed for Saddam Hussein's survival to this point. There was, throughout the war, a clear consensus the United States should not include the conquest of Iraq among its objectives. On the contrary, it was universally accepted that our objective was to push Iraq out of Kuwait, and it was further understood that, when this was accomplished, combat would stop."[21] Briefly, a speech that began by reflecting what most Democrats were feeling was then shown to portray Gore as having been both dishonest and ill advised, as ever, an enigma.

Gore's party, too, behaved enigmatically, as if it planned to recapture power by stealth. However, since 9/11 the caution of Democrats—their reluctance to criticize Bush on almost any issue—had been remarkable. In the run-up to the November 2002 elections, they complained that the White House staccato on Iraq had muffled issues like the flagging economy, on which the Democrats had said they wanted to campaign.

Actually, the issue was there for them, less resonant certainly than it might have been but not muffled. Still, it might as well have been, since they didn't try very hard to establish it. Their message on taxes, for example, continued to be feeble and ambiguous.

They could have cleared the air and done themselves a favor by connecting a war in Iraq to the heavy damage to the economy that would probably ensue. One day after the election, the Federal Reserve Board cut interest rates by half a percentage point, to 1.25 percent, citing "greater uncertainty" that is "currently inhibiting, spending, production and employment."[22]

In general, Democrats failed to speak with a clear voice about any issue or convey a sense of purpose, or demonstrate that they stood for anything. And, of course, this voicelessness damaged a party whose credibility was far from robust. "The Democrats thought they could run against President Bush without actually running against him," wrote E. J. Dionne Jr. right after the election.[23]

Many and probably most Congressional Democrats were opposed to granting Bush an authorization to use force against Iraq more sweeping than any past resolution conferring such power. But they were fearful of being perceived as weak on a security issue, especially with an election just a few weeks off. Bush seemed to be turning up the pressure. In a speech on October 7, just before the scheduled vote, he said, "Iraq could decide on any given day to provide a biological or chemical weapon to a terrorist group or individual terrorists. Alliance with terrorists could allow the Iraq regime to attack America without leaving any fingerprints."[24]

That same day, George Tenet sent a letter to Congress that took a different line on Iraq and terrorism. In both the letter and testimony to Congress, the CIA argued that Iraq would not take the "the extreme step" of assisting terrorists in attacking the United States with weapons of mass destruction if Washington did not invade. Iraq, the agency observed, has little reason to provoke Washington to march on Baghdad.[25]

But three days later, despite the reassuring language from the CIA, just twenty-two of the Senate's fifty Democrats voted against the resolution. And among those voting for it were the handful who aspired to their party's presidential nomination. Three of their colleagues who voted no were campaigning for reelection, and each won by a substantial margin.

A less sweeping alternative resolution was put forward by their deeply respected colleague Carl Levin of Michigan, who was then chairman of the Armed Services Committee. His version didn't authorize the use of force on a strictly unilateral basis, thus meeting one of the chief objections to the White House draft. Still, only twenty-four Democrats voted with Levin, and those who voted against it included the presidential hopefuls who seemed determined, at least on this issue, to appear more like Republicans than members of an opposition party. Very probably, they were looking ahead to the presidential primary season that would begin in little more than a year.

A majority of House Democrats voted against the White House resolution, even though their leader, Richard A. Gephardt, another presidential aspirant, threw all his weight behind it. The vote in the House was 296 to 133.

At this same time, a task force on homeland security put together by the Council on Foreign Relations recommended a half dozen or so major initiatives designed to prevent terrorist attacks or reduce their effects. The co-chairmen, former Senators Warren B. Rudman and Gary Hart, described these steps in a newspaper article in which they also said something about Iraq (and which was published on election day): "Collectively, the president and congressional leaders must restore the same degree of urgency and immediacy to securing America that they devote to war in Iraq. Indeed, war in Iraq should be initiated only when the United States is fully prepared to deal with the potential serious domestic consequences of undertaking that war."[26]

Concern with these consequences helps explain why some skeptics, the ones who doubted the genuineness of Bush's commitment to invade Iraq, concluded wrongly that it was all bluff—a major exercise in psychological warfare aimed at generating a military coup in Iraq. "There's all kinds of ways to change regimes," Bush told reporters without elaboration after the meeting with Tony Blair at Camp David on September 7.[27]

To the extent that a strategy of bluff was under way, a high point was reached in early January 2003, when the Bush administration leaked a list of fourteen names, including that of Saddam Hussein, specifying who would be removed from office and tried as criminals. This gesture was interpreted as inviting senior Iraqi personalities not listed to move against the regime and thereby earn some credit. Iraq's military was on notice from Washington that commanders who ordered the use of chemical or biological weapons against American or allied forces would be held to account for war crimes.[28]

An argument that moderates had hoped would sink in was that Saddam could be deterred. He invaded Kuwait in August 1990 because he read the signals from Washington, not unreasonably, as conveying indifference. But when faced with the prospect of losing the first Gulf War, he did not use unconventional weapons. Since then, the argument ran, he hadn't seen indifference and hadn't tempted fate, except for threatening Kuwait again in 1994; he backed off when the Clinton administration responded militarily.[29]

We should not invade Iraq now, many argued, because there is no reason to do so. The same people who said that Saddam couldn't be deterred were many of those who had been saying that North Korea couldn't be deterred, even though deterrence actually had worked in the Korean peninsula over a half century. And North Korea could be more threatening and capable of greater mischief than Iraq.

Splits existed within every political faction, including the hard right. Some of its members who opposed invading Iraq may have been mainly worried about jeopardizing relations with oil-producing states, notably Saudi Arabia. On August 21, the *Financial Times* reported that "disgruntled Saudis have pulled tens of billions of dollars out of the U.S., signaling a growing disenchantment with America." Banking estimates of the total withdrawals ranged between $100 and $200 billion.[30]

Within a month of the Security Council's approval of Resolution 1441, the issue of whether a second resolution would be required was in play. Timetables were a problem. Bush was impatient. He and most of his advisors wanted to start the war no later than early March 2003, if only for weather-related reasons. However, to establish a material breach of 1441 the inspectors would have had to demonstrate that Saddam had both concealed information and failed to cooperate with them. Accomplishing that could have required more time.

Hans Blix, the chief weapons inspector, noted correctly that 1441 did not establish a deadline and that the team would need more time. He argued that in any case he had more time; he did so by drawing on language from an earlier resolution—the one that had created the inspection teams.

"Saddam is in an iron box," declared a study released by the Carnegie Endowment for International Peace in January 2003. "With tens of thousands of troops around Iraq, an international coalition united in support of the inspection process, and now hundreds of inspectors in the country able to go anywhere at any time, Saddam is unable to engage in any large-scale development or production of chemical, biological, or nuclear weapons. It would be exceedingly difficult to import significant quantities of proscribed materials or to manufacture longer-range missiles or missile components."[31]

According to the report, the inspectors had only just begun to use advanced or high-tech equipment. They arrived in November and did not use their first helicopter until January 5, 2003. In mid-January they were less than halfway through reinspecting the more than 700 sites that UNSCOM—the previous UN inspection agency—had identified. They estimated that it would take another year to complete the inspections.[32]

The problem that for years had most worried the cognoscenti—Iraq's on-and-off quest for nuclear weapons—was sure to be clarified by the inspections process, that is, if it had been allowed to run its normal course. Between 1991 and 1998, UN inspectors destroyed Iraq's nuclear program, and it hadn't been rebuilt. An authoritative article that appeared in February 2003 said, "With an embargo in place and inspectors at work, Iraq is further from a nuclear capacity than at any time in recent memory."[33]

That conclusion may have been based on a report from the International Atomic Energy Agency (IAEA) to the UN Security Council in late January 2003. According to IAEA Director General Mohamed El Baradei, "We have to date found no evidence that Iraq has revived its nuclear weapon program since the elimination of the program in the 1990's."[34]

Blair badly needed a second resolution that had majority support. If one or more permanent members of the Security Council blocked the measure, he would have been ready to go to war alongside Bush, or so he indicated. But first he had to schedule a debate in the House of Commons on the issue and then a vote. It would amount to a vote of confidence in his government. Without a second resolution Blair could be expected to win, and he did. But whether he could remain on course with Bush and avoid serious political injury to himself and the government was far from certain.

Blair also needed something more—a coating of diplomatic accomplishment that might offset the cannonade of protest to the war. More exactly, he needed a believable commitment from Bush to begin building peace in the Middle East around the creation of a Palestinian state. Again, however, Blair lost his only chance of prevailing when he didn't tie British support for the war to agreement by Bush to undertake a broad and evenhanded approach to the much bigger and more urgent problem.

Early in 2003, Bush sounded impatient, suggesting strongly that inspections led nowhere; that the time for removing the problem forcibly lay just ahead. Blair, on the other hand, wanted another eight or so weeks to try to rally Britain to the cause and improve prospects for a second resolution.

The distance between Washington and other European capitals widened. On January 17, Russia signed three agreements with Baghdad for exploration and development of oil fields in southern and western Iraq. Two days earlier, the Russian government said that it saw no reason to consider war. But Putin's position was regarded as fluid, and the betting was that in the end he would be "on side." A day later, however, Chancellor Schroeder said that not only would Germany not take part in any "military intervention in Iraq, but that is exactly how our voting behavior will be in all international bodies, including the United Nations."[35]

The next day it seemed to get worse. With Colin Powell present, Dominique de Villepin, France's foreign minister, told the UN in unusually blunt terms that France would not support any Security Council resolution for military action against Iraq in the weeks ahead. France, he said, didn't rule out the possibility of using its veto power if the United States pressed the council to authorize war against Iraq for failing to disarm.[36]

Powell had been blindsided and embarrassed. He was furious. As he and other moderates saw things, the French had undercut them and the case for exercising patience. What had occurred, they thought, would leave Saddam all the more resistant to coming clean. "It was barking mad," said an angry British diplomat. Powell abruptly fell in line with hawkish sentiment. "Iraq's time for choosing peaceful disarmament is fast coming to an end," he said. "Inspections will not work." Three weeks earlier, he had urged patience with Iraq and argued that the UN's weapons inspectors needed more time.[37]

Rumsfeld elected to respond to these European defections with a curious dismissiveness that left many people, even some in the administration, scratching their heads. France and Germany, he said, were "old Europe. If you look at the entire NATO Europe today, the center of gravity is shifting to the east." Rumsfeld and many of his colleagues often believe what they want to believe. If told that France and Germany command more influence on the continent than all other European countries combined, they would doubtless shake their heads.

Bush had problems in Europe that he and his team didn't see. One is that he has very few working relationships with Europe's leaders. Bush talks on the phone with some regularity to Blair, Putin, and Italy's Silvio Berlusconi, as well as occasionally to Spain's José María Aznar. He rarely speaks to any of the others. And when he does talk to a European counterpart, he usually wants something, and the other party doesn't learn much.

Even Blair is told less than he could reasonably expect to hear. He never learned, for example, what Bush was planning to do about coping with sources of instability post-Iraq. "The prioritization of the post-Saddam agenda isn't clear," said a senior British official a few weeks before the war began. "We don't know whether it will be India-Pakistan, North Korea, Iran, Afghanistan, the Middle East, or what. Blair was offered no clue." He was referring to the meeting between Bush and Blair on January 31. But even with the war under way, Blair was offered no hint of Bush's intentions toward other troubled places.

The administration, it seemed to some European governments, was bent on dividing them—turning differences within the EU into deep and perhaps long-lasting rifts and setting back efforts to develop a cohesive, institutionally connected union of states. In many capitals, Bush was seen as signaling with his conduct and his doctrine that he alone could decide where a threat to the world order might lie and what would be done about it. Also, his administration's misleading and unconvincing efforts to connect Iraq to al-Qaeda probably deepened the split with Europe. Colin Powell, the most trusted of Bush's advisors, tried and failed to establish the link at the Security Council six weeks or so before the war began; he, too, was losing credibility.

Europe's chattering classes assumed quite wrongly that the administration's idée fixe was about colonizing Iraq and seizing oil, not about disarming Saddam and/or removing him. In turn, the administration didn't grasp the nature or the depth of Europe's opposition to the war, to Bush's policies, or to Bush himself. Americans living or traveling in Europe got used to reproachful people saying, "It's not you, it's him."

Bush aside, Germany's opposition to the war drew on a culture of pacifism that developed after the last great war. France's more overtly hostile posture had multiple sources, apart from Bush himself. Some of these were connected: notably, the visceral threat from al-Qaeda; the presence in France of 6 million Muslims, many of them isolated or alienated from the French mainstream; Bush's support for Sharon and his indifference to the Middle East peace process.

Also, Chirac, who has led a charmed political life and is a moth to the spotlight's flame, saw an opportunity to assert

French leadership in Europe, especially with Germany, the inherently stronger power, being weakly led by its chancellor and unable to wield the same weight in the Security Council as France, one of five permanent members and thus endowed with veto power. Its status at the UN sharpens France's commitment to an institution-based world order, although Germany's commitment to that order is at least equally strong. However, Chirac got carried away, not for the first time. He seemed to see himself dueling with the American *hyper-puissance*, holding the line against this pretender to a unipolar world. He and Bush seemed to take equal pleasure from being on a collision course with the world looking on. But in promising to veto a second UN resolution, whatever its terms, Chirac was threatening to scuttle a process that he himself had done much to set in motion just a few months earlier.

Blair tried to sustain the process. He wanted diplomatic cover for a decision to invade that had been made a year earlier; and since his party and country were insisting on a multilateral solution, he had more at stake than the others. The French and Russians wanted to buy time by giving the UN renewed authority to remove Iraq's WMD from the scene. But the issue, as seen from the White House, was always about regime change. WMD was a pretext, as Ari Fleischer, the White House spokesman, made clear in a press briefing. "It's disarmament and regime change," he said in reply to a question about whether Saddam Hussein could avoid war by "completely and totally disarming."

Diplomacy never really had a chance. Blair fought his corner bravely, but he was trapped between Bush's hubris, Chirac's vanity, and his own overcommitment to the role of Washington's junior partner. He was the big loser of the prewar diplomatic battles. He had to work a lot harder than Bush to mobilize support and neutralize opposition to the war, and he paid a far higher price; he lost two cabinet members and a measure of credibility. Yet in return for supporting the war and taking huge political risks in doing so, Blair got nothing of consequence.

Two months after the war, Philip Stephens noted in a column in the *Financial Times* that Bush's and Blair's motives in Iraq were not quite the same. "Mr. Bush," he said, "takes his Christianity from the Old Testament; Mr. Blair prefers the New. The president is out to defeat the forces of darkness, the prime minister to shine light into the world. For Mr. Blair, the moral good of deposing a dreadful regime fused with the strategic ambition of a new world order."[38]

In ways large and small, the administration was inflicting serious damage on America's relations with allies and its standing in the world. Cheney was seen by diplomats as being the dominant influence on policy and Rumsfeld as the blunt instrument. Just before distinguishing between the old and new Europe, Rumsfeld told a largely European audience at a conference on security in Munich that France and Germany faced diplomatic isolation with their opposition to the war; that "diplomacy has been exhausted, almost"; that the UN was on "a path of ridicule"; and that NATO could be headed the same way.[39] Diplomacy, of course, had been all but exhausted, not by Europeans but by the administration's aversion to it. By then, Bush was being seen in Europe, and in most of the rest of the world, as a bigger problem than Saddam Hussein. In his curiously inept campaign to gain support for the second resolution, Bush managed to lose Mexico, the only country that he ever showed any interest in or tried to cultivate.

There was talk in much of Europe that the United States, besides overplaying its hand, could be drifting toward imperial overstretch. Bush and his inner circle stigmatized dissent. By early March 2003, he had described other countries as "being with us or with the terrorists" ninety-nine times since taking office.[40] His blend of a jingoist national security policy, massive tax cuts, and mammoth deficits were seen as inviting the sort of trouble that can take root.

Laura d'Andrea Tyson, who chaired Clinton's Council of Economic Advisors, wrote:

> Not withstanding its unilateralist claims that America's destiny should not depend on decisions made by an 'illusory international community,' the White House is implicitly assuming that the rest of the world will foot a sizable share of the bill.
>
> The U.S. already absorbs about 5 percent of the world's savings. It borrows about $200 million from the rest of the world each day to cover its savings gap. The Bush budget will increase that gap to as much as 9 percent of gross domestic product by the end of the decade. Will the rest of the world be willing to cover a gap of this size and, if so, on what terms? There is no reason to think the U.S. will find itself in a buyer's market. Indeed, there are already worrying signs that foreigners are beginning to reduce their massive holdings of dollars and dollar-denominated assets.[41]

On January 28, Bush devoted a major part of his State of the Union address to Iraq. With muscular language he sought to rally a jittery public behind the war. He said little that was new, but did repeat at least one allegation that some of the people around him had to know was seriously misleading. Saddam, he said, "aids and protects terrorists, including members of al-Qaeda [and] could provide one of his hidden weapons to terrorists, or help them develop their own."[42] Despite closely held intelligence reports pointing the other way, Bush, Rumsfeld, and others continued to tell it like they thought it ought to be. Indeed, by the time the war began on March 19, polls showed that more than half the country thought that

Iraq was responsible for 9/11. The hard right was doing what comes naturally—using the means at hand to justify the ends it seeks.

Other governments could and did explain why Saddam's Iraq would have had every reason not to help al-Qaeda or any sibling group. First, these shadowy, elusive groups hated Saddam. Second, and more important, they can't be controlled. Yet they can commit acts of terror that would in turn invite retaliation against a more accessible target—a pariah state like Iraq to which they were connected. Saudi Arabia and Pakistan are in a different category. Saudi Arabia did, of course, sustain al-Qaeda for a time, but its singular and special relationship with the United States has thus far spared the kingdom serious difficulties in Washington, although that may change.

Pakistan, a nominal ally, is the only country that fits Bush's profile of wicked behavior and imminent threat. Two of its provinces are controlled by Taliban and al-Qaeda sympathizers. For now, there may be little that the Musharraf government can do about the chaos and anarchy in parts of the country. But it can and should be held to account for its remarkable decision to make possible North Korea's highly enriched uranium program. Pakistan, on its own initiative, provided program parts: weapons design, gas centrifuges, materials to make centrifuges, data of the sort that would enable the customer to avoid having to test its devices.

Besides the alleged link between Iraq and al-Qaeda, Bush's speech contained another even more ominous but equally misguided passage in which Saddam was reported to have tried to buy large quantities or uranium oxide from the West African nation of Niger. The report was based on forged documents. Whether any of Bush's aides knew that wasn't clear. The story itself had been known within Western intelligence circles, including the CIA, since late in 2001, and by the following year had been discredited. The hard but unavoidable question is, When did Bush's staff know the documents were counterfeit, before or after the speech? And Bush himself? Perhaps significantly, Powell's strong portrayal of Iraqi misconduct to the Security Council a week later contained no mention of the uranium oxide tale.

The febrile tone and content of Bush's message left little doubt about his intentions toward Iraq. But he hadn't answered, either convincingly or rigorously, the obvious questions: Why the haste? What about al-Qaeda? The Middle East? The interplay of North Korea and Pakistan? The prospect of another India-Pakistan war, with its fearful possibilities?

Nor were there answers to the questions that hadn't yet been asked. Bush was heading into a conflict without having told the country about the likely costs—financial and political—that would begin to accumulate once the predictably swift combat phase had been completed. Who would share these costs with the United States? What countries would make up the occupation force and what about the duration of that phase? How would the costs of first waging the war and then repairing the damage to Iraq be financed? What administrative arrangements were being planned and what would the UN's role be?

A few weeks before the war began, General Eric K. Shinseki, the U.S. Army's chief of staff, told the Senate Armed Services Committee that "something on the order of several hundred thousand soldiers" would be needed afterward to "control ethnic tensions and provide humanitarian aid." The committee chairman, Senator Carl Levin, said, "There's no way we can keep 200,000 troops in Iraq for a substantial time." Others were quick to point out that Shinseki was saying that unless allied forces were also involved, peacekeeping would involve all or most of the deployable army."[43]

A day later, Rumsfeld and Wolfowitz scaled back Shinseki's estimates in no uncertain terms, while a few other officials privately came to his defense. Shinseki's testimony was regarded by many Pentagon watchers as expressing the concern of the uniformed military that the war on Iraq had not been thought through. In private, several senior officers worried aloud that the post-conflict phase had to be as methodically planned as the war itself. That had not been done, they warned.

The United States could well be left to pick up most of the tab for a war that could cost $100 billion or $200 billion, according to Lawrence Lindsay, Bush's first economic advisor.[44] This allegedly high-end estimate caused distress at the White House and may have contributed to Lindsay's departure not long afterward. Mitchell Daniels, who was director of the Office of Management and Budget, said that Lindsay's projections were too high, even though various institutions outside the government made similar calculations. The cost of the war against Iraq in 1990–91 was estimated at $61 billion, of which the United States paid just 10 percent. (Most of the funds were contributed by Kuwait, Saudi Arabia, the United Arab Emirates, Japan, and Germany.)

Bush's budget for fiscal year 2004 didn't cover the costs of war in Iraq or of occupation, humanitarian aid, and reconstruction. And in Washington various officials explained that Iraq would have to pay the price of reconstruction. Some loose talk about oil came directly from the White House. Various European officials who visited Washington shortly before the war began inquired about the administration's plans for financing the postwar phase. That would be paid for with Iraq's oil money, they were airily told by Elliott Abrams, who was put in charge of planning the post-Saddam era as special assistant to the President for Near East and North African affairs. Abrams had acquired some notoriety for his role in the Iran-Contra affair in the late 1980s.

Other officials hinted privately that Iraqi oil revenue would be used to rebuild the country. And five days before the war began, Colin Powell took this line public, saying, "We're going to use the assets of the people of Iraq, especially their oil assets, to benefit their people."[45]

By chance, a very different opinion was put forward in a report issued by two prestigious institutions at this time. "There has been a great deal of wishful thinking about Iraqi oil, including a widespread belief that oil revenues will help defray war costs and the expense of rebuilding the Iraqi state and the economy," it stated. "Notwithstanding the value of Iraq's vast oil reserves, there are severe limits on them both as a source of funding for post-conflict reconstruction efforts and as the key driver of future economic development. . . . It is important to stress that Iraqis have the capability to manage the future direction of their oil industry. A heavy American hand will only convince them, and the rest of the world, that the operation against Iraq was undertaken for imperialist, rather than disarmament reasons. It is in America's interest to discourage such misperceptions."[46]

In his last meeting with Blair before the war, Bush agreed to say something about the Middle East peace process, and he did—in a speech delivered a few weeks later, on February 26. He said, "If the terror threat is removed and security improves, [Israel] will be expected to support the creation of a viable Palestinian state. . . . As progress is made toward peace, settlement activity in the occupied territories must end."[47]

However, Bush provided no specifics. Who would judge whether the terror threat had been removed or sufficient progress toward peace had been made? If the recent past was any guide, Bush would let Prime Minister Sharon make those calls. British officials made little effort to hide their skepticism and frustration.

Bush used the speech to try signaling sunny prospects for democracy post-Saddam. "A new regime in Iraq," he said, "would serve as a dramatic and inspiring example of freedom for other nations in the region." But on the very day of the speech, the State Department circulated a classified report that sharply took issue with the line that regime change in Iraq would lead to democracy there and elsewhere in the region. A copy of the report, which had been sent to a small group of senior officials, was then leaked to the *Los Angeles Times*. It was labeled "Iraq, the Middle East and Change: No Dominoes."[48]

An early, if not the first, casualty of the war was the failure of talks on the Cyprus problem—talks that had been under way for eighteen months, and had offered much the best chance of resolving a dispute that has often had Greece and Turkey at daggers drawn and complicated the effort to enlarge the EU. The Greek and Turkish communities have been divided since 1974. Their leaders have always opposed a deal. But this time, the implacable opposition of Rauf Denktash, the Turkish leader, could probably have been overcome by the new and more forward-leaning Turkish government. In that case, the Greek Cypriot resistance to a settlement was expected to collapse. But at the eleventh hour, Turkey's government, under pressure from its military, drew back; and on March 10, just nine days before the war began, the deal collapsed. Turkey's military, although not in principle opposed to the deal, wanted to avoid a distraction of this kind in the run-up to the impending war in Iraq, which had its full attention.

In considering the baneful effects on Europe and Euro-American relations of the misadventure in Iraq, Turkey was a good place to begin. Since the Korean War, it had supported U.S. military actions, in part because Washington had always been careful to avoid making unreasonably large demands or being insensitive to Turkish interests. This time Washington made unrealistic demands and displayed indifference to the interests of a country where most of the population—an estimated 94 percent—opposed war in Iraq. Who lost Turkey could become a question embedded in the postmortems of the second Gulf War.

.   .   .

One of Richard Perle's principal allies in past battles during the Cold War era was the newspaper columnist Robert D. Novak. However, on the twelfth of the seemingly endless but tumultuous month of August 2002, Novak drew wide attention with this comment: "Richard Perle . . . at the moment terrorists struck Sept. 11, laid out a strategy enjoying strong support in the Bush administration: the United States, aligned with Israel against Islam and the Arab world, with the removal of Hussein even more important than pacifying Afghanistan."[49]

Early in the run-up to the Gulf War of 1991–92, some diplomats in Washington and at the UN took comfort from a line of thinking that went as follows: this first post–Cold War crisis should be a blueprint for the future; Americans can't resolve it alone, must have help, and will continue to put a premium on cooperation with Moscow and on strict coordination of policy within the UN. That line of thinking was traceable to the then national security advisor, Brent Scowcroft. But nothing came of it; nor, in its present form, is anything likely to come of it now. Another opportunity to strengthen the international system and, with it, regional stability may just slide away all but unnoticed.

Bush steered the country's strong commitment to waging war on terrorism and chaos toward the less urgent but more accessible target, Iraq. And people on all sides worried that removing Saddam would become phase one of a process. However, an implicitly large beneficiary of an unsanctioned campaign aimed at wholesale regime change in the Middle East and Persian Gulf would be Osama bin Laden and his legatees (if bin Laden is dead). Their purpose—indeed, their raison d'être—is to divide the West from Islam, starting with the Arab world. The strategy associated with several administration personalities, including Perle, Wolfowitz, Cheney, and Rumsfeld, could, if adopted, serve to achieve that goal.

In their relentless push for war and against sensible policy, this group of ultras corrupted the intelligence process, and risked bringing further trouble to the Middle East, chaos in Iraq and a commitment there of uncertain scale and duration, terrorist acts on U.S. soil, turbulence in world financial markets, and lasting damage to major institutions. In sum, the risks of going to war with Iraq were much clearer than the administration's declared reasons for waging one.

CHAPTER 3

Iran in a Bad Neighborhood

Tax cuts aside, President Bush's strongest commitments have been aimed at removing Saddam Hussein from the scene and building a national missile defense. Neither project was seen abroad or by most of the intelligence community at home as responsive to an imminent threat. Beyond the tight circle of Bush and his advisors, the focus of concern was Southwest Asia and Northeast Asia, especially the failed states—Pakistan and North Korea—that are most likely to unhinge the security of their neighbors and the stability of the world.

Pakistan is the most threatening of them—first, because it is congenitally turbulent, a breeding ground for terrorism and barely governable; second, because it lies within the single most unstable region; and third, because it has nuclear weapons. If Pakistan is the largest problem, Iran could be the key to regional stability. Iran is the best positioned and best equipped of countries to discourage the widening band of terrorism, much of it rooted in Pakistan. In a region that lacks so much, including leadership, and doesn't like what passes for authority, Iran has attributes that distinguish it from all its neighbors: It has rudimentary but real politics based on free elections. It has a legitimate government. Iran is a country with its own history and natural borders, not borders laid down by diplomats and fixed by treaty. Pakistan has many more people, but Iran, with 66 million, is next. Iraq has 22 million.

What's more important is that Iran's citizens are the region's most civilized and accomplished, a reflection of their traditions and history. Iran has played a role in Southwest Asia similar to the one France had for centuries in continental Europe. Persian culture radiated through the region, including India in its swath. Persian was the lingua franca of the region's educated class, just as the French language was in most of Europe.

In the hours and days after 9/11, Iran presented Washington with a huge opportunity. Overnight, reformist president Mohammed Khatami and his allies acquired leverage that allowed them to think in terms that would have seemed fanciful the day before. And the steps they took then to support the United States in its campaign against al-Qaeda and the Taliban reflected a shift in the balance of power in Tehran. Popular support for the new path was impressive. In many Iranian cities, observances in sympathy for the American victims of the attacks were held.

The *Wall Street Journal* reported that demonstrations "involving tens of thousands of men and women in several cities all took place after World Cup–qualifying soccer matches. Instead of mere rallies for the national team, the gatherings have echoed with catcalls against the Islamic clerics who swept Shah Reza Phalavi from power in 1979. . . . For a regime that has staked its Islamic credentials on confronting the 'Great Satan' America, the specter of a pro-U.S., pro-secular opposition arising among Iran's youth is a nightmare."[1] Also, Iranian assistance played a large role in American successes in Afghanistan and in the formation of an interim government in Kabul.[2]

It was then that the Bush team could and should have begun to support the efforts of the reformers to nudge Iran in a direction compatible with American interests. However, Washington politics got in the way of these interests and, indeed, of common sense. The hard-liners around Bush were determined to align American policy with that of Ariel Sharon and his Likud party, who were bent on identifying Iran not just as a threat to peace and stability within the region, but as the major threat. Vincent Cannistraro, a former chief of CIA counterterrorism operations, has said that since Bush's axis of evil speech, "the Iranian hardliners . . . have clearly eclipsed the pragmatists under Khatami and have stepped up arms shipments and aid to Hezbollah, as part of an effort to open a 'northern front' to support the Palestinian resistance."[3]

Neither the American nor Israeli hard-liners would concede even a degree of difference between radical mullahs and reformers. The leadership of Israel's Labor party governments once took a very different view. Yitzhak Rabin and Ehud Barak regarded Iran as a strategic ally in waiting.

Although Iran remains an emotive topic among Americans, it will eventually dominate the Persian Gulf, and the United States will have to adjust to that. But the great divide in today's Iran isn't just the existential standoff between hard-liners and reformers; it also involves a stagnant economy and sweeping unemployment. And the American sanctions that hobble the economy provide Washington with leverage that would be useful when and if bridges to the reformist bloc are built.

Lifting the restraints on Iran's economy would create another source of energy at a time of energy uncertainty, and would create the transparency that large investors require. Hard-liners in Tehran will resist change of this kind, but won't be able to do so indefinitely if the change goes forward at a measured but steady pace.

But nothing of the sort is likely to happen unless and until

Washington replaces truculence with sensible, pragmatic policy, thereby giving the reformist bloc the freedom to maneuver that it had fleetingly post-9/11. Bush's people say, in effect, that they admire Iran's people and will work closely with them once they have thrown off the "unelected few" who run things.

The line was formalized in July 2002 when Bush took the unusual step of issuing a policy pronouncement, not from the White House or the State Department, but in his own name, thereby underlining the importance of the statement. It broke with a process that had gone on for five years during which Washington had tried fitfully to work with the Khatami government. Bush and his advisors, according to one official, had decided that the reformers were "too weak, ineffective and not serious about delivering on their promises." Instead, this official said, "we have made a conscious decision to associate with the aspirations of Iranian people. We will not play . . . the factional politics of reform versus hard line."[4]

Reform versus hard-line disputes were on display throughout that summer and fall. In June, Tehran turned over sixteen suspected al-Qaeda fighters to Saudi Arabia, with the understanding that any intelligence that emerged from their interrogation would be passed on to Washington. An Iranian spokesman put the event "in the context of Iran's commitment, within the framework of international law to fighting terrorism." But not long afterward, Ayatollah Khamenei, Supreme Leader of the Revolution, reacted to Bush's pronouncement on Iran by comparing him to Hitler.[5]

By May 2003, various members of the Bush team, starting with Rumsfeld, were bent on confrontation with Iran. The main attention-getter in the indictment of Iran, as reported in a flurry of newspaper articles, sounded very like what he and others had said about Iraq just one year earlier—that al-Qaeda militants were being sheltered. Besides making that charge, Rumsfeld also accused Iran of trying to influence political events in Iraq. The *Financial Times*, as well as various journals, reported that he was "spearheading efforts to make 'regime change' in Iran the official policy goal of the Bush administration." In the same article, George Tenet, head of the Central Intelligence Agency, was described as having "contested" Rumsfeld's allegation about the link between Iran and al-Qaeda.[6] That, too, was reminiscent of the year before and the clash then between intelligence agencies and the Pentagon leadership over Iraq.

In Washington, administration hawks regard Iran as a pre-revolutionary society. They convinced themselves some time ago that change in Iraq would light a match in the region and release pressures that would transform Iran, first by ridding it of the radical clerics and then by creating a model democracy.

Most Iran watchers disagree, arguing instead that the country's largely dissident society is capable of exercising restraint and already possesses basic attributes of democracy. Yes, they say, a strong reaction to repressive tactics could spill over into the streets, but probably won't. The mullahs can't risk provoking violence on a scale that could lead to revolution. Their priorities are less about preserving the purity of the revolution than about staying on. They are, by and large, corrupt politicians determined to cling to power for as long as possible, if only because the longer they stay the more they can steal. Meanwhile, they will allow some liberalization of the economy so as to relieve the pressure for serious change.

Iran sits astride major transit routes for the export of oil and natural gas, whether by sea or overland through Central Asia. It constitutes the land bridge connecting states of the Middle East to emerging states of Central Asia.

Iran has relations ranging from good to normal with most of these states, thanks to Khatami, who regarded his country's past policies as unnecessarily confrontational. "Making enemies is not a skill; real skill lies in the ability to neutralize enemies, convert animosities to human interactions and scale down hostilities. . . . And, this is not incompatible with our principles," he has said.[7]

Although the principles alluded to are those on which this Islamic republic is based, there are radical differences among its leaders about how to apply them. Ayatollah Khamenei describes the world as a "jungle . . . everything we do is a battle. Life is a battlefield." Iran, he says, should cultivate "loneliness" and retain a closed system.[8] Khamenei and the rest of Iran's inner circle of mullahs control the army, the police, and the intelligence agencies.

These hard-liners are supported politically and, for now, financially by the *bazaaris*, the merchant class. And while they control the levers of power, their need for a workable and efficient government affords Khatami some leeway. He tries to draw strength from broadly based support for his moderate and creative approach both to domestic and regional issues and to external relations. In the 1997 election, he got 70 percent of the popular vote; in June 2001, he was reelected with 71 percent. In parliamentary elections a year earlier, the "reformist" bloc that supported Khatami won close to 200 of the 290 seats. Over 69 percent of the eligible voters cast ballots in that election. Both the economically distressed middle class and the swollen student population support the reformers.

They drew hope from the Khatami government. Hundreds of newspapers, magazines, and journals began to appear. Restrictions on art and literature, as well as dress codes, loosened.[9] Among Khatami's first steps after becoming president was ending Iran's self-imposed isolation from the Arab states in the Persian Gulf, along with efforts to subvert these states. He then began actively improving relations with Iran's neighbors, equating this activity with expanded access to markets and economic growth.

Khatami's government also took care to develop good and productive relations with West European countries. Although the step was part of the effort to reconnect Iran to the world, Khatami also wanted to discourage any prospect of the United States and Europe jointly mounting a hostile policy toward Iran. Prior to his arrival on the scene, differences, a few of them serious, between Iran and some European countries had led to EU ambassadors being recalled "for consultations."

Opening Iran conforms to the interests of the hard-line mullahs for whom survivability of the Islamist regime is the first priority. They've seen the need to re-engage the world, and they gave up trying to export revolution some time ago.

But these extremist elements still use American policy to justify an antagonistic approach to matters of importance to both countries and to excuse Iran's underperforming economy. They continue to demonize the United States—the "great Satan"—and to support terrorist attacks against Israel. Their line is: The United States cannot be trusted; it wants to control and exploit Iran. Thus, we must challenge the United States on all fronts—Afghanistan, the Arab world, Central Asia, and so on. The question is, how to respond? By strengthening the Khatami government, argue European leaders, who are determined to help the reformers allay the threat from al-Qaeda and sibling groups.

Iran, unlike its neighbors and the Arab states, is well positioned to take on these groups whose inspiration is both political and ideological. The political component is largely a reaction to American policy. The more serious and rooted component is ideological. It attracts people driven to carry out terrorist acts in response to warped interpretations of religious duties.

The conflict with Iran's enemy, the Taliban, offered reformers an opportunity to join the war against terrorism. The radical clergy, however, judged the war in Afghanistan as a campaign to kill Muslims. The two parties have taken polarized positions. For the reformers to be seen as gaining the upper hand, even gradually, would send a very strong signal to Islamic societies everywhere, starting with Arab countries. Iran's extremists could then be directly challenged at home, and that is what the reformers, including most members of the Majlis, Iran's parliament, want to make happen.

The Bush team's current view of Iran is very different from that of every U.S. ally in Europe. The Europeans see Iran as the region's strategic pivot, the one country that could make a serious difference in Southwest Asia, provided it had the support of the other country that could make a difference—the United States. Europeans regard Washington's current policy as willfully myopic, especially in its failure to comprehend the possibilities offered by the reformist government of a people who, unlike their neighbors and the states of the Middle East, are largely pro-American, committed to democracy and a free press, moderate in their style and attitude, and opposed to terrorism. Most Iranians (about 70 percent) favor normalized relations with the United States, but Washington's line puzzles and troubles them. "We're trying to move from ideology to modernity, and Bush is moving from modernity to ideology," a student leader was quoted as saying.[10]

Chances are, the society will drift, but at a snail's pace, from political stalemate to fundamental change of a kind and on a scale that the reformist bloc seeks to create. It is not a question of if but when. The mullahs are fighting for their own survival but are doomed by forces they can't control, starting with demographics. Iran is often described as the world's youngest country: 65 percent of the population is under the age of thirty. Another basic threat to the insular clerics is the society's access to the world via the Internet and the abundance of computers along with satellite dishes that bring distant television broadcasts into residents' houses and apartments. These advantages do not exist elsewhere in the region, at least not to nearly the same degree.

The children of Iran's revolution are at least as politicized as their predecessors and a lot more measured and worldly.

They, like members of the Majlis, are distancing themselves from the revolutionary cant and asking aloud whether Iran's interest lies in becoming the last great enemy of the world's only superpower; and whether it lies in being the last of those who cry death to the Zionist state and support terrorist actions against it.

In the mid-1970s, a sharp decline in Iran's agriculture provoked a flight to the cities, putting heavy pressure on employment and in turn on the regime. The war with Iraq created a second migrant wave from the villages to the cities. Today, the population in Tehran is just over 12 million, close to one fifth of the country.

The losses in the war with Iraq were staggering and drove women into the labor force. Women are now seriously politicized. But all of the country's young want change, if only for protection against the mullahs, who are not foolish enough to kill student leaders but do not hesitate to make ordinary, lower-profile activists disappear.

In December 2002, a well-informed piece in *Newsweek International* said:

One of the catalysts for the current unrest has been an important political shift within the student unions, or *Anjoman Eslami*, that played a key role in ousting the Shah. Composed largely of ardent Muslims, the unions have led large protests at several Tehran universities and in other cities like Isfahan, Shiraz, Urumiheh and Tabriz, where they've decried the regime's Potemkin democracy. Breaking a taboo, some students have directly criticized Supreme Leader Ayatollah Ali Khamenei. . . . The widening rift in the religious community seems to have Khamenei worried: at a Dec. 6 prayer meeting, he implored the country's clerics "to refrain from criticizing one another."[11]

What the society mainly needs is leadership. By 2002, it was becoming clear that Khatami and the other senior members of the reformist bloc had produced less change than promised. Support for the reformist government was in a steep decline. The restless students were giving up on Khatami, who, even if basically well-intentioned, remains in their view a creature of the system. He seemed strongly inclined to a reformist agenda so long as it didn't upset the extremist clergy. Questions arose: Was Khatami a leader or a mere symbol of pressure for change? A Gorbachev-like figure, inviting change but not making it happen? He came under pressure to break the stalemate and set a pace for political reform.

Khatami bowed to the pressure in August 2002 by delivering an ultimatum to the Ayatollah Khamenei. Unless the supreme leader approved legislation that would strengthen Khatami's hand by neutralizing two key pillars of the power structure—the judiciary and the Council of Guardians—Khatami would resign as president and take his administration and most of the parliament with him. He denounced the prosecution of scores of political activists and the closure of many newspapers. Closed trials without a jury, he declared, were unconstitutional. And in a televised press conference, he said, "These are not empty slogans. . . . I intend to defend the rights of the people." He then alluded to the country's frustration and unhappiness, saying, "I accept there is a sort of hopelessness in our society."[12]

It was a showdown. The Majlis seemed certain to pass the controversial legislation, as it did, and the Council of Guardians, an appointed upper house that vets laws and parliamentary candidates, seemed certain to veto it, as it did. A large question loomed. Was the greater part of the society on a collision course with its rulers, and, if so, would one side wobble and seek compromise?

Earlier in the summer, a popular history professor named

Hashem Aghajari was arrested in Tehran after expressing doubt in a speech that only the clerics were competent to interpret the Koran, Islam's holy book. "Are people monkeys to imitate clerics blindly?" he asked. He also proposed a Shia version of Europe's Protestant Reformation. Aghajari was convicted of blasphemy and on November 6 sentenced to death.

But almost at once the supreme authority seemed to wobble. Ayatollah Khamenei ordered a review of the death sentence, even though, according to law, the sentence would have to be appealed before it could be reviewed. But Aghajari refused to appeal and seemed content to martyr himself on behalf of a freer society. There ensued a wave of protests, the most widespread in years.

Three weeks after the sentence was handed down, four student leaders were arrested. The next morning they were set free on the orders of the Supreme National Security Council. Had an actual test of strength begun, as the signs seemed to suggest? Probably not. The reformers were pushing a little harder against the existing political tolerances, and the mullahs were cutting them some slack. They were determined to force Khatami to withdraw the troublesome legislation, whereas he appeared to be determined to redress the balance between elected institutions—the presidency and the Majlis—and the insular, anachronistic hierarchy. In turn, the reformist bloc showed it wouldn't be intimidated. In late May 2003, more than one hundred reformists, including members of the Majlis and political prisoners warned the ruling mullahs that the gap between them and the people might lead to "the fate of the Taliban and Baghdad regime."[13]

But neither side was ready for the dispute to spill into a battle for the streets between the *basij* (militia) and the young. Iran had a revolution without imploding, as any other country in the region would have done; it doesn't want to repeat that experience.

Iran has become hard to read. The pro-reform public is alienated. It wants change, but cannot find an instrument of change it can rally to. The reformers were beaten soundly in national municipal elections, held in February 2003; the vast majority of reformers didn't vote.[14] Still, it would be a mistake to read much significance into that event. The earlier victories of the reformers at the polls and the latent, if unguided, force they represent have shifted Iran's political balance, probably permanently. The children of the revolution, as Shahram Chubin has written, have "largely become alienated by the incompetence, repression, corruption and rhetoric of the leadership."[15] And so far, this leadership has been understandably reluctant to take on the forces for change and modernization in an actual test of strength.

During the Cold War, Washington kept Russia out of the Persian Gulf. However, the Clinton administration reacted to the radical mullahs by adopting a policy toward Iran and Iraq called dual containment. Its unintended effect was to smooth Russia's return to the Gulf. Now Russian companies profit from contracts that U.S. firms are denied by their government's policy. Gradually, other governments began to question the utility of a policy aimed at isolating both of the Persian Gulf's major players. However, Clinton's advisors were concerned chiefly with Iran's unconventional weapons programs, especially the likelihood that with enough help from Russia, Iran would develop a nuclear fuel cycle. But after watching Khatami and his reformist bloc win successive presidential and parliamentary elections, the Clinton team began to hold low-key private talks with emissaries of the reformist government. Up until 9/11 and for a short time thereafter, the Bush administration followed suit. But contact was broken off after Bush anathematized Iran in January 2002.

Although Iran and the United States have enemies in common, they do continue to have serious differences. Overcoming these won't be easy. For Washington to restore diplomatic relations, Iran would have to agree, first, to end its opposition to the peace process in the Middle East; second, to close off financial and other support of organizations involved in terrorist attacks against Israel; and third, to pin down its pledge to forgo development of nuclear weapons.[16]

Iran's larger interests are clear. It wants to be treated by the United States as a normal place and a respectable player within the international system. It urgently needs help with economic development. It confronts a serious demographic imbalance and must create employment for its youthful population. More than half of Iran's college graduates are unemployed. Normal relations with the United States would improve Iran's access to capital markets and World Bank loans. Monetary claims left over from the past could be settled.

Above all, Iran needs Western investment in its oil and natural gas fields. In exploiting new oil fields, its government wants to work with American companies, such as Chevron Texaco, Conoco, and Exxon Mobil, instead of being limited to their European competitors. But U.S. sanctions forbid all such ventures, even though the prohibitions are not enforceable against non-American oil companies, and U.S. counterparts are thereby denied a level playing field. American opposition to a productive role for Iran in the Caspian is yet another divisive issue.[17]

Prior to 9/11, a U.S. initiative designed to rebuild fences with Iran would have started with exchanges on the less sensitive issues. But if, as George Perkovich has observed, "the aim is to persuade Iran to abandon interest in acquiring nuclear weapons, Washington will need a strategy to convince Iranian nationalists that their country will gain security, respect, and a prominent role in post-war politics in the Persian Gulf."[18]

Indeed, the reformist government's vulnerabilities and the dangerous neighborhood that Iran inhabits may together argue for taking, or trying to take, a long first step in that direction, one designed to narrow, if not settle, differences over the dominant issue: security. For example, the UN Security Council could adopt a resolution that would guarantee Iran's security against unprovoked aggression from an external force; such a step would directly connect the United States and Russia and other permanent members of the council to that purpose.

A lot would be required of Iran in return for so broad a guarantee, including a cessation of support for groups such as the Palestinian Islamic Jihad, Hamas, and Hizbollah and of opposition to the peace process. (Hizbollah has been described by some American authorities as terrorism's "A-team," and Iran provides one of its training bases as well as financial support.) Iran would be obliged to ratify a recent and broader protocol laid down by the International Atomic Energy Agency (IAEA) that is designed to ensure detection of covert efforts to develop nuclear weapons. To date, Iran has been judged in compliance with its obligations to the IAEA, but is nonetheless suspected, doubtless correctly, of covert movement toward a nuclear weapons option. Iran defends its reluctance to accept more intrusive inspection rules on the grounds that its access to civilian nuclear-reactor technology is restricted, mainly by the United States. But that restriction would presumably be dropped if Iran accepted the full-scope IAEA protocol.[19]

The Khatami government might elect to pay the price for a package of this sort. The question is whether Iran's real rulers would let that happen or instead find themselves unable to resist the explicit pressure that came with a Security Council resolution that bore the signatures of each of the Permanent Five—China, Russia, the United States, Britain, and France.

The argument for developing nuclear weapons resonates. Pakistan, which has nuclear weapons, lies to one side; Iraq wanted them, may one day want them again, and used chemical agents against Iran; Israel, a formidable, if undeclared nuclear power, is in the neighborhood. Its strategic link with Turkey worries Iran, as does the heavy American military presence in the Gulf. To the south are the Saudis, another potential source of instability.

Iraq no longer poses the threat that it once did. Whether the threat offered a sufficient reason for Iran to possess nuclear weapons was debatable. Some Iranians felt that the United States would not have removed Saddam Hussein's regime by force if Iraq had acquired nuclear weapons. Hence, Iran should have them, too. And as one Iran watcher has written, "The bitter memories of the eight-year war, in which Iranian territory was occupied, its population terrorized and its economy devastated, continue to haunt Tehran and condition its strategic outlook. Having lost approximately 20,000 of its citizens to Iraqi chemical-weapons attacks with little outcry from the international community, the Iranian leadership is largely unified around the necessity of maximizing its deterrent capabilities."[20]

Israel's nuclear weapons are held up by most Iranians, whether reformers or hard-liners, and by most Arabs as a shining example of American hypocrisy. Washington, they observe, regards WMD, especially nuclear weapons, as forbidden fruit unless deployed by Israel. Iran's extremists argue that American policy is based on Israel's having a monopoly on nuclear weapons in the Middle East and Persian Gulf.

Iran's reformers and hard-liners both support the Palestinian resistance. But the reformist bloc doesn't link the issue to the country's national security and favors limiting Iran's role to moral and ideological support of the Palestinians. "We will honor what the Palestinian people accept," said Khatami.[21] It's the clerical establishment that insists on rejecting the peace process and providing direct material support to the major Palestinian rejectionist groups. But even Khamenei has said that Israel is too far away to become Iran's jihad.[22]

Iran and Pakistan are very different. Iran, of course, is predominantly Shia, whereas Pakistan's tribes are Sunni. And their stylistic distinctions, though less important, are striking. The cities of Iran are alive with coffeehouses and Internet cafés, where self-confident, animated young people talk about reform and improving their lot. They exude creativity and style. Pakistan, by comparison, exudes pessimism and a sense of foreboding. Iran's students and reformers, unlike their Pakistani counterparts, are not afraid of extremist elements.

Although the issues that divide Tehran and Islamabad have never reached the level of crisis, relations have worsened in recent years. Pakistan's heavy involvement with the Taliban is partly responsible. The Taliban is a bone in Iran's throat. Pakistan's Islamic schools, the *madrassas*, have become training grounds for terrorist and other radical groups throughout the Muslim world.[23] An increase in sectarian abuse of Shia minorities located near Pakistan's border with Iran is among the serious irritants.

Of even greater concern to Tehran is the prospect of Pakistan's internal turmoil spiraling out of control and spilling over into neighboring territory. A triangle in northwest Pakistan that borders Iran and Afghanistan is suggestive of that concern. It consists mainly of bandits and opium fields, and is called "Dopistan" in American intelligence circles. The region was once part of the kingdom of Afghanistan, and the inhabitants, who are mostly Pashtun, call themselves Afghan. In 1998, Pakistan severely tried Iran's patience by testing a nuclear weapon in Baluchistan, just thirty kilometers from Iran's eastern border; the event caused a parliamentary deputy and several prayer leaders to call for the development of nuclear weapons.[24]

Twice in the year that followed 9/11, Pakistan and India, which share a border that stretches 2,912 kilometers, nearly went to war. Most capitals assumed, cautiously, that neither party would cross the nuclear threshold. That was and remains a shaky assumption. Pakistanis know that they will lose another war fought only with conventional weapons.

Their government provokes anger as well as concern for several reasons, not least its decision to export nuclear weapons technology to North Korea, which had already launched a worrisome commerce between the two by selling Pakistan ballistic missile technology. This mutually exploitable traffic has raised questions about the U.S. alliance with the government of President Pervez Musharraf, who, of course, helped in ousting the Taliban and pursuing terrorists, many of them Pakistani grown or trained. His support for the war in Afghanistan cost him, because it angered Pakistan's religious parties. His vulnerability increased when it became clear that he would have elections that could not threaten his power. If Musharraf were deposed and replaced by a radical regime, India might overreact. And so might Washington.

Musharraf has cast his lot with the United States, but he needs the support of his military, Pakistan's only solid and modern institution. He will have its backing only so long as his regime can hold its own against the country's inner turbulence and the overall decline that set in some years ago.

Keeping his military on a tight rein is made difficult by its preoccupation with the threat from India. To cite just one example, in July 2002, American intelligence agencies, according to a *New York Times* report, tracked a Pakistani cargo airplane as it landed in North Korea and took on a payload of ballistic missiles, North Korea's chief export. The airplane, ironically, was an American-built C-130, part of a force that Musharraf had assured Bush would be used to hunt down members of al-Qaeda. American intelligence has observed several other examples of this commerce.[25] And despite Musharraf's stand against the Taliban and al-Qaeda, his army still provides terrorist groups operating inside the country with training camps and weapons.

Moreover, the war against al-Qaeda and its Taliban host pointed up disturbing uncertainties about Pakistan's nuclear weapons. We know too little about them, and we hear divergent views from people with special knowledge of the problem. We don't know exactly how many weapons Pakistan has deployed; estimates based on somewhat sketchy information point to thirty-five or so. Nor do we know where some of them are actually stored. We don't know whether weapons are kept separately from delivery vehicles. Exactly who in Pakistan possesses that knowledge, including the whereabouts and security of fissile material, is also unclear. Pakistan is secretive because it worries that external forces, starting with India, might want to take control of or destroy its nuclear arsenal.

A widely but cautiously held view is that the weapons themselves are secure so long as General Musharraf's government can prevent upheaval and remain in power. Another rather widely held but equally cautious opinion is that the government has staying power. Still, it hasn't inspired confidence, and what would happen in the event of its overthrow is the major uncertainty, hence the major concern. Inevitably, there has been talk of "exfiltrating" Pakistan's nuclear weapons in that event, a possibility that most people with special knowledge regard as implausible. Former Deputy Secretary of State Strobe Talbott has said, "I doubt that we know where everything is that we would be going to exfiltrate or extract [and it would be] dangerous because it would almost by definition be in conditions of political instability when there would be a lot of potential for violence."[26]

Whether terrorists, even with a background in nuclear technology, could assemble and activate a Pakistani nuclear weapon is unclear. Pakistan's weapons, unlike America's and Russia's, are presumed to lack devices of the kind that prevent warheads from being armed unless various codes are punched in. Some U.S. officials have spoken of transferring such devices to Pakistan in order to enhance the security of the weapons. Others oppose such a step, arguing that it would encourage Pakistan to deploy weapons now kept in pieces for safekeeping. Instead, the argument runs, the United States should help only by providing better surveillance equipment, thereby improving physical security around Pakistan's nuclear weapons sites.[27]

India aside, Russia is probably at least as concerned with Pakistan's alarming instabilities as any nation. Putin has made that clear to Bush privately, and he also did so publicly in November 2002, just after NATO leaders, meeting in Prague, had agreed to take in seven new members. Bush flew to St. Petersburg to meet briefly with Putin, who had asked for the stopover partly because he wanted to tone down domestic criticism of enlargement and of himself for not opposing it.

When they met informally with reporters just before Bush was due to leave for the airport, the focus was not on the Prague meeting but on terrorism and Iraq. Bush cited the arrest of a senior al-Qaeda figure as evidence of progress in the campaign against terrorism. But then Putin surprised reporters, and possibly Bush, by raising pointed questions about the roles of major American allies—Pakistan and Saudi Arabia—in the campaign. He asked, "What can happen with weapons that exist in Pakistan, including weapons of mass destruction?" He has privately referred to its military leadership as "a junta with nukes."[28]

Putin is known to doubt the reliability of Pakistan as an ally. He noted that Osama bin Laden is believed "to have taken refuge . . . somewhere between Afghanistan and Pakistan." Locating him, he observed, was a major piece of unfinished business, even though the administration's focus was on Iraq.[29]

China shares the concern about Pakistan but also some of the responsibility for its nuclear weapons. Pakistan's bomb is a copy of China's. Moreover, the materials used to build Pakistan's ballistic missiles are Chinese, although the technologies are North Korean. China, Russia, and the United States will have to assume some responsibility for the overall problem of Pakistan by working together cooperatively. That has not happened, and it might not be enough. There is no clear path through the political minefield that Pakistan has become.

The security of Pakistan's nuclear weapons would be even more worrisome if Iran, too, found its way into the nuclear club and thereby added to the region's uncertainties and underlying instabilities. Iran is openly developing ballistic missiles, which it says are essential to deterrence. However, its nuclear weapons program is convincingly described as "clandestine, illegal and potentially subject to political debate, contention and reversal."[30]

The reformers in Tehran are less impelled than the ruling establishment to develop unconventional weapons. They have a less threat-driven view of the region and the world. However, it is unlikely that this bloc would agree to give up any unconventional weapons project, whether chemical, biological, or possibly even nuclear, without a broad security guarantee such as the one described above. Indeed, most Iranians regard having these weapons in some form as essential to their defense. They saw their country invaded by Iraq with the support and encouragement of the United States. As the Iraqis attacked them with poison gas, they felt that the world, including the United States, turned a blind eye to the scene. Worst still, Washington abetted the outrage by supplying Iraq with intelligence for targeting.

Still, Iran is a more stable and secure place than its neighbors, and its leaders know that. They themselves call it an "island of stability."[31] The low-grade threats that do concern them—drug smugglers and refugees from violence on Iran's frontiers—do not require sophisticated weapons, let alone weapons of mass destruction.

The risks associated with acquiring nuclear weapons have focused a serious debate in Iran's press and foreign-policy community. The strains of moving ahead with the program would put a strain on the country's economy. Also, the political, economic, and strategic costs to Iran of violating its commitments to the nuclear Non-Proliferation Treaty (NPT) or withdrawing from the treaty would be heavy.[32] Various moderates have pointed to the dangers of provoking the Americans by crossing this red line and doing so for no compelling reason.

Still, signs that surfaced early in 2003 seemed to suggest that Iran might be moving its still embryonic nuclear program closer to this red line. International inspectors visiting a town called Natanz in late February were shown a small network of centrifuges for enriching uranium. And they learned that Iran had acquired components for making a great many more centrifuges. Iran has insisted that the activity at Natanz is devoted strictly to making fuel for a civilian nuclear power program.[33] But numerous Iran watchers, European and American, now take a skeptical view. Chances are that Iran's rulers are creating an option to develop nuclear weapons when and if they see the political balance of pluses and minuses as shifting to that side. Their reading of that balance may depend on whether Washington can abstain from heavy-handed tactics aimed at regime change in Iran.

Iran resembles a cubist painting, elusive and multifaceted, defying swift or easy comprehension. It is both contradictory and deceptive, enough so that virtually any point of view about any topic can be defended. For example, the calculations that lie behind Iran's nuclear weapons are unclear, partly because it's far from certain that the program, a very slow-moving one, can or will reach its presumed destination. What is clear, however, is that Iran won't be able to develop the weapons without continued and substantial technological assistance and training from Russia. Equally clear is the corrosive impact of this assistance on relations between Washington and Moscow.

The Clinton administration started complaining in the mid-1990s when it noticed several Russian agencies and aerospace firms helping Iran to build an intermediate-range ballistic missile, itself a knockoff of North Korea's Nodong system. Washington could hardly complain to Tehran, not just because there is so little contact between them, but also because the United States "grandfathered" India's and Pakistan's nuclear weapons and has always turned a blind eye to Israel's; and these exceed the combined total of Indian and Pakistani nuclear weapons.

However, the United States has never ceased pressing Iran's major suppliers of nuclear technology, notably China and Russia, to break off this traffic. And in 1997, China essentially did so. First Clinton and then Bush tried to discourage Russian work on Iran's Bushehr nuclear power plant and key fuel-cycle technologies.[34] But Boris Yeltsin wouldn't stop it.

By early 1995, according to one authoritative account, "the U.S. discovered that the Bushehr plant was only the tip of the iceberg. In a secret protocol to the January agreement, the Russian Ministry of Atomic Energy (Minatom) had agreed to supply Iran with key fuel cycle facilities . . . including . . . a uranium enrichment centrifuge plant. Washington was furious. Either the Russian government had lied about the extent of its nuclear relationship with Iran or Minatom was making extraordinarily sensitive commitments without Moscow's knowledge."[35]

Well before Clinton left office, the dispute had become the

single most contentious post–Cold War issue between Washington and Moscow. Since then, it has been no less contentious but far more conspicuous, since, excepting Iraq, Bush and Putin haven't had other issues to quarrel about seriously.

Russia is the one country that in recent years has had good relations with not only the United States, but also Iran, Iraq, and North Korea. In Iran, it has priority interests. Moscow needs stability throughout Southwest Asia as well as in Central Asia, the region in which terrorism and organized crime intersect. Whether Bush got Russian support in coping with these persistent threats to security would depend on whether he met Putin halfway. Iraq was less important to Russia than Iran, which, like Russia, opposed the Taliban in Afghanistan and Sunni Muslim fundamentalists in Central Asia. But Putin hadn't wanted Iraq dealt with unilaterally. He had hoped to be part of the decision-making process, if only because whatever happened in Iraq would affect Iran and regional stability. Putin had to worry that if the United States went after Iraq, Iran might in one way or another be next. And he had to reckon with a large body of Russian opinion that sees the United States as running amok. He cannot be viewed as approving the use of force by the United States against Russian interests. These interests are heavily engaged in Iran.

Bush has tried, so far unsuccessfully, to bring Putin around to U.S. thinking about the dangers of an Iranian bomb, especially one mated with a ballistic missile. Exactly why Putin has resisted heavy pressure on this issue is uncertain. After all, post-9/11, he began yielding to Bush on other issues that were expected to be contentious. These included further enlargement of NATO, cancellation of the ABM Treaty, and Putin's apparent acquiescence on the related and even more sensitized issue of national missile defense. Putin couldn't have prevented any of these moves by Bush, but he could have openly opposed them and thereby helped himself politically at home.

Instead, he elected to stand down and build on his rapport with Bush.

The importance to Putin of bonding with Bush, although hard to exaggerate, needs perspective. Russia cannot become a player in the world's, or Europe's, affairs without a strong economy. So Putin must use his opening westward to embed Russia's economy in the world economy. (Russians are tired of hearing their economy compared to Schleswig-Holstein's. Actually, it is the Netherlands' economy that is slightly larger than Russia's.) But rebuilding the economy also requires earning money. Iran is one of the few places where Russia can earn serious money, even if doing so agitates its tie with Washington.

Russia doesn't have much to sell apart from weapons and energy. Oil and natural gas account for about 55 percent of Russian income from trade, military sales for about 5 percent. But the arms sales have a multiple role. They are controlled by the Kremlin, which skims off a large sum to finance political campaigns.

A weak economy and the absence of domestic demand for energy and weapons have obliged the government to sell these products elsewhere. In doing so, it wants and expects to have a free hand. Russia confronts worrisome problems in Eurasia, and in Central and Southwest Asia. Putin can take the position that if Russia helps to protect the interests of NATO members in these regions, its Western partners should do no less for Russia. But for Washington, selling nuclear reactors to Iran is a red line that Minatom continues to ignore.

Russian national security policy is struggled over by competing lobbies. There is no coherent national security apparatus except on paper. In fact, there isn't much actual foreign policy, because the bureaucracy is very weak. If Putin makes a decision and then stands behind it, the decision is likely to be carried out. Otherwise, the process tends to be chaotic. ("Shambolic" is the term used by one Russianologist.) Large financial interests work closely with other governments and with foreign commercial interests. In Iran, Minatom can be the dominant influence on whatever Russia does, or doesn't do, because there is no alternative view in Moscow.

Minatom is in league with the weapons-makers and military leaders who sell arms to China, India, and Iran. In pressing for the reactor sales, this lobby argues that Iran has never supported the Chechen rebels; also, that whereas the United States had been unconcerned with what happened in Afghanistan prior to 9/11, only Russia and Iran prevented the Taliban from conquering the whole country.

This argument appeals to a body of opinion that wants to downgrade relations with the United States. It argues that Russia should not act like a vassal of the United States, expresses concern about being humiliated by it, and argues that Putin has gotten far too little for the concessions he has made to Bush.

A much smaller and very different lobby supports Putin's efforts to link Russia with the Western system. This group is joined by powerful, all-but-independent oil interests that are trying to attract U.S. investment and want a larger share of the U.S. market. They have no interest in good relations with Iran. They have an issue with Iran over the division of the oil in the Caspian Sea. There are allegedly elements within this lobby that wouldn't object to seeing Iran become a nuclear power if that meant its permanent estrangement from the United States.

Minatom itself operates with great authority, so much so that it has been called a state within a state. It deploys its own independent foreign policy and unlike most parts of Russia's bureaucracy has an independent financial base. By one well-informed account, "there is no effective government oversight of Minatom programs and no evidence that contract revenues make their way to government revenue accounts. Increasingly, there are reports of corruption, disappeared funds, and scientists providing knowledge beyond the contracted and monitored work at Bushehr [which] poses a proliferation risk by contributing to Iran's knowledge for developing an independent fuel cycle for producing weapons-grade fuel."[36]

Shortly before the summit meeting between Bush and Putin in May 2002, the issue of Russian nuclear assistance seemed for a moment to have been settled. Both Bush and Tony Blair were informed by Putin that he had seen the light and would go no further in assisting Iran's program. But then Putin reversed course and reneged publicly. In his joint news conference with Bush, he refused to confirm assurances that Bush had claimed to have just heard from him in private. And in July, Russian officials revealed plans to build as many as five more reactors after current work at Bushehr was completed.[37] Five months later, Minatom's president, Alexander Rumyantsev, announced that Russia was ready to begin delivering nuclear fuel to the Bushehr power plant.[38]

The erratic course of this issue suggests that while Putin runs a much tighter ship than Yeltsin, he, too, may on occasion be thwarted by powerful interests determined to protect gainful arrangements and hostile to the explicit pro-Western thrust of his policy. In this case, Washington must ask itself where the larger U.S. interest lies. Is it with continuing to hold Putin's feet to the fire even if that expedient hasn't worked any more than it did with Yeltsin?

Chances are, Putin could halt this technical assistance to Iran provided he could point to benefits for Russia that would more than balance its losses. These benefits could be both economic and political. Celeste Wallander sees U.S. interests as being harmed when Russian policies are driven by short-term economic benefits. "It is in U.S. interests," she writes, "to help Russia's political and economic leadership focus on its long-term objectives because these offer greater benefits. A single contract with Iran that benefits Minatom is not worth as much as joint development of new oil fields and pipelines, which has beneficial effects not only for oil companies but also the Russian economy and government budget."[39]

Moscow would find this kind of approach more persuasive if it were accompanied by an American political initiative designed to make an unstable region less dangerous. Specifically, the United States ought to climb down from its lonely, self-defeating attitude toward Iran, align its policy with that of its allies, and set about building bridges, large or small, to Iran's reformers.

Chapter 4

Red Lines

Besides lacking a popular mandate, George W. Bush arrived with less perspective on the past, distant or recent, than most newly minted presidents. What he brought was a set of strongly held opinions arising from one man's take on moral clarity. What he didn't bring was the one attribute that an incoming commander-in-chief must have—an interest in knowing what he doesn't know.

Bush's natural style leads him, with an incautious boldness, to tackle problems that don't directly threaten the United States. He could, for example, support Israel's self-injurious treatment of Palestine at no apparent cost to America's national security; and he believed, or was led to believe, that the price to be paid for ending Saddam Hussein's dominion was reasonable.

North Korea was a very different matter. First, the price for going where the moral clarity lay was unreasonably high; second, Bush's obsession with Iraq skewed the administration's focus; third, the onset of a political crisis threatening peace and stability on the Korean peninsula obliged the White House to take account of what neighboring countries—Japan, China, South Korea, and Russia—were saying.

The earliest, largest, and most recurrent splits within Bush's circle involved Northeast Asia, especially China and North Korea. Several administration figures, including Rumsfeld and Cheney, were from the start ready to establish China as an adversary, real or potential. Condoleezza Rice characterized China as a "strategic competitor, not the 'strategic partner' the Clinton administration once called it."[1] The State Department chose instead to recommend treating China as a strategic partner, notably in trade. It had allies, not always potent, in the Treasury and Commerce Departments and the Office of the Special Trade Representative. The military services were divided. The air force favored the hard line on China, the country against which America's newest high-performance aircraft—the F-22—was mainly developed. The army was less drawn to the hard line perhaps because it had fought a war that involved Chinese as well as North Korean forces.

Gradually, the State Department's softer line acquired support in the White House. Rice's characterization of China was not repeated. The events of September 11 tempered the discord between Washington and Beijing and edged aside their differences over Taiwan and national missile defense. China helped in persuading President Musharraf to bring Pakistan into the anti-Taliban coalition.

As China became a more serious player in the world's affairs and moved closer to the United States, the Bush line became roughly similar to what Clinton's had been. Bush's arms-sale package to Taiwan included submarines for the first time, although Taiwan hadn't pushed to acquire them. Yet the Bush administration did not approve the sale of some high-performance systems that Taiwan really did want.

With North Korea, the administration's line was hard from the start and powerfully expressed one of its canons: when possible, avoid any endorsement or emulation of Clinton-era policies, attitudes, and practices. Into the discard went Clinton's so-called No Hostile Intent declaration worked out with North Korea in October 2000. The all-but-completed broad agreement aimed at settling differences involving North Korea's advanced missile programs was gone. Instead, the administration elected to start over and separate the issues.

Into one basket went the so-called Agreed Framework of 1994 that froze North Korea's nuclear weapons program; into another went the sensitive issue of ballistic missile development. The Bush people also raised the issue of conventional forces, a move that was as foolish as it was gratuitous. Apart from their military function, the regime relies on these forces to help maintain internal security. And, of course, the administration had no intention then of altering the U.S. force posture in the peninsula. Last, but hardly least, was the insistence that everything had to be agreed to before anything was agreed.

Unfriendly states that deploy unconventional weapons tend to be seen by at least part of Washington's national security bureaucracy as a threat to the territorial United States. Typically, however, their programs are part of a deterrent strategy directed primarily against old neighborhood enemies and, secondarily, against American forces in the region.

North Korea falls into that category. And it should be seen for what it is—a feudal autocracy—insular, paranoid, deeply insecure, possessing only the bare rudiments of an economy. But this so-called hermit kingdom deploys the world's fifth-largest army and has the knowledge and capacity to build an arsenal of nuclear weapons.

North Korea's insecurity has for decades driven its attitude toward the world beyond. Its neighbors—China, Japan, and South Korea—are seen as potential aggressors and implacably hostile. But the leadership, however irrationally, feels that the most acute and imminent threat emanates from Washington. How then to assure survival when the immediate adversary is a superpower, indeed the only superpower?

In coping with Washington, the regime rarely says what it means. It relies instead on a mix of brinkmanship and ambiguity. "They are not inclined to speak clearly," says a former American intelligence official who dealt with North Korea over a period of time. "They are hard to understand. Sometimes they take someone aside just to say something that cuts through all the verbiage."

In the early 1980s, Kim Il Sung, the "Great Leader" and father of the current leader, Kim Jong Il, decided that a serious flirtation with nuclear weapons would send the strongest possible message to Washington. He authorized his government to develop a program that drew on atomic energy reactors located at Yongbyon. In December 1985, the Soviet Union agreed to supply four light-water reactors, provided Kim Il Sung would join the nuclear Non-Proliferation Treaty.

Nearly twenty years earlier, he had tried and failed to persuade Mao Zedong to share China's nuclear knowledge.[2] Ever since, China has regularly made clear its disapproval of North Korea's apparent quest for nuclear weapons, fearing, for example, that Japan, South Korea, and possibly even Taiwan would follow suit. Moreover, North Korea has great strategic significance for China. It doesn't want to look across the Yalu River and see a unified and, who knows, capitalist Korean state, least of all one with nuclear weapons. But China, North Korea's chief supplier of food and fuel, has rarely used its undoubted leverage to influence the regime's behavior.

As China sees it, only the United States can modify this troublesome conduct. But Washington and Beijing have a tendency to talk past each other on matters concerning North Korea. Each party likes to think that only the other can nudge Pyongyang in the right direction. It has been said by some specialists that North Korea is the only part of the world where China underestimates its influence. That may be, but Beijing has always worried that its leverage with North Korea, once used, would be spent and not available at a time when the stakes might be higher.

Problems involving the Korean peninsula preoccupy Chinese leaders more than other international issues. Only the remote possibility of Taiwan declaring its independence would be seen in Beijing as a graver threat than a conflict on the peninsula. The presence of nuclear weapons in North Korea might invite such a conflict. At a minimum, it would create instabilities and probably a major world crisis. North Korea might collapse altogether, sending floods of refugees streaming into China. Many have already arrived. Beijing's leaders also worry that North Korea may resume testing ballistic missiles, thereby causing the United States to deploy a theater missile defense that would probably cover Taiwan.

Actually, North Korea's penchant for the diplomatic highwire act, although troublesome, proceeds from a tough, uncomplicated logic. Scott Snyder of the Asia Foundation has described the regime's behavioral pattern this way: "North Korea uses guerilla tactics to demonstrate alternatives to negotiation and to impose costs on the larger party for not negotiating. Instinctive reliance on such strategies has preserved its very existence, leveled the playing field with more powerful neighbors and allowed North Korean negotiators to punch above their weight. North Koreans are sticking to the playbook because it has historically worked."[3]

North Korea wants above all to put to rest its insecurity and concern for the survivability of the regime by negotiating a nonadversarial link with the United States. And it hopes for an end to political and economic isolation. It distrusts each of its neighbors, but the United States, although at least equally distrusted, is seen as the pivotal force—the one and only player in this high-stakes struggle who can provide the security that North Korea is playing for. China, Japan, South Korea, and Russia share this assessment.

What the Pyongyang regime wants first from Washington is a nonaggression guarantee in some form, something in writing but less formal than a treaty which, the regime knows, could not be ratified. A nonaggression guarantee would work, as would a commitment to full normalization of relations. North Korea also insists that Washington cease interfering with its efforts to acquire help from international lending institutions and other governments. North Korea has become an aid-dependent country.

Track one of Pyongyang's two-track approach to Washington is the "guerilla tactic"—using nuclear and ballistic missile technologies to build advanced weapons programs. Pyongyang is normally ready to walk back these programs when and if Washington is willing to move at least part of the way in its direction. So far, it has been a tit-for-tat process, neither more nor less. In short, North Korea's programs exist mainly to be sold. And if Washington isn't buying, they can always be sold commercially. Ballistic missile technology is not just North Korea's leading cash crop, it is virtually the only one. And if Washington won't pay the political price for shutting down the programs, North Korea's leadership is ready to treat them as insurance policies—meaning that the regime would actually deploy advanced ballistic missile systems and possibly nuclear weapons as a hedge against whatever military threats to the state, real or imagined, loom on the horizon. The military bureaucracy is believed to have pressed hard for developing *and* deploying nuclear weapons not for bargaining purposes but strictly on grounds of security.

In the past, North Korea would slow down or halt movement on track one when it got too close to one of Washington's red lines. That happened in 1989 when the administration of President George H. W. Bush concluded that North Korea was violating the NPT by reprocessing nuclear material. The administration secured a de facto trade by taking steps that

North Korea had pressed for: The United States withdrew nuclear weapons from the Korean peninsula, cancelled the annual joint U.S.–South Korea military exercise, and arranged a high-level meeting with North Korean officials. For its part, the North Koreans agreed to allow inspections by the IAEA of its nuclear facilities.[4] Not long afterward, North and South Korea agreed jointly to ban nuclear weapons from their countries.

The ensuing calm—a sense that North Korea was ready to shelve its nuclear program—didn't last long. Not long after the process began, the regime began blocking inspections of suspect facilities. In 1993, the CIA reported that the North Koreans might have obtained enough plutonium from fuel rods to make one or two bombs. Orbiting American satellites with high-resolution cameras provided pictures of efforts to deceive inspectors. This material was shared with the IAEA and presented to a closed session of its board in February of that year. The board demanded that North Korea allow a special inspection of the sites in dispute.[5]

The stakes were now very high. "The credibility and international standing of both the IAEA and North Korea were at risk," wrote Don Oberdorfer, whose history of the recurrent crises on the Korean peninsula is the authoritative text.

> If the IAEA could not secure international backing for inspections when there was evidence of cheating, its newly asserted authority could be defied with impunity. . . . For Pyongyang, the danger was this would be only the first of increasingly intrusive inspections it regarded as masterminded by hostile U.S. intelligence. Also at risk was the sensitive issue of respect, what Koreans call ch'emyon and Westerners call "face," a matter of tremendous, almost overwhelming, importance to the reclusive North Korean regime. "For us, saving face is as important as life itself," a senior North Korean

told Representative [Gary] Ackerman during his visit to Pyongyang.[6]

The timing could not have been worse. The administration of President Bill Clinton had been in office for just a few weeks, and South Korea had just acquired an even newer government. Then, on March 12, North Korea raised the stakes by threatening to withdraw from the NPT.

The world reacted with shock and dismay. The issue of North Korean nuclear weapons shot to the top of the international agenda.[7] Months of stalemate and shrill comment ensued. Efforts to resume inspections became a circular process leading nowhere, and there was talk of war.

North Korea was still ready, at least in principle, to swap its nuclear arms program for the political assurances it wanted from Washington. But that meant pressuring the Americans by keeping alive the program and maneuvering close to the brink. The concern was that Pyongyang might fail to recognize the brink and stumble over it. The United States and its allies urged the UN Security Council to adopt sanctions against North Korea. Pyongyang warned repeatedly that "sanctions are a declaration of war."[8]

The Clinton administration was being tugged in different directions. With the crisis growing more acute, it wisely decided to name one official to manage negotiations with Pyongyang. The choice was Robert Gallucci, assistant secretary of state for political-military affairs. Gallucci had a technician's grasp of nuclear matters and broad experience with the politics of arms control.

Years later, Gallucci compared the spring of 1994 to Barbara Tuchman's account of events in the summer of 1914 in *The Guns of August*. The Korean crisis, he felt, "had an escalatory quality that could deteriorate not only into a war but into a big war."[9]

Among the advocates of sanctions and a generally hard line

were those who felt that the North Korean state, if pushed, would collapse altogether. William Perry, who was secretary of defense at the time, didn't share that view but did see the prospect of war becoming more acute. At issue was the future of 8,000 fuel rods that could be unloaded from the reactor at Yongbyon and from which plutonium could be separated, enough probably for four or five nuclear weapons. A move by North Korea in this direction would have been a casus belli, as Perry wanted to make clear. He favored drawing a red line in the form of coercive diplomacy that included the threat of military force. Specifically, he hinted that North Korea's nuclear facilities might be bombed, but that the United States favored negotiating a removal of the threat they posed, or trying to. President Clinton backed him.

The planets were now aligned, more or less. The last thing North Korea wanted was another war with the United States. An outline of the bilateral arrangement with the United States that it craved had emerged. Hence, the regime agreed to close Pandora's box if Washington would provide the necessary guarantees, plus some material aid. In October 1994, the trade was formalized in the Agreed Framework, which embodied the first nonhostile relationship ever between the United States and North Korea.

Negotiations about controlling weapons are always lengthy and arduous, and this one had been no exception. However, the interests of North Korea's neighbors were heavily engaged; Japan and South Korea, American allies, worked side by side with Washington in developing the U.S. position. And at an early stage China made the deeply counterintuitive move of applying direct pressure on Pyongyang. North Korea's leadership was quietly told to accommodate world opinion on the nuclear issue or confront the prospect of UN sanctions that China was not prepared to veto. It didn't hurt that Clinton had just announced that he would grant U.S.-most-favored-nation trade status to China without attaching human rights conditions.[10]

A curious but pivotal role was played by former President Jimmy Carter. In the early 1990s, Kim Il Sung occasionally invited Carter to visit Pyongyang, although each time the State Department urged him not to go on the grounds that his visit would probably do more harm than good.[11] In June 1994, with the Clinton administration flirting with sanctions against North Korea, Carter did travel to Pyongyang as a private citizen, not as an emissary. Informal talks had produced the outline of an agreement based on a freeze of North Korea's nuclear weapons program in return for some material assistance. But Kim Il Sung had not been made aware of this exchange until he met with Carter, who persuaded him to make a deal with Washington along these lines. Then, with North Korea's leader having accepted this informal arrangement, thanks to Carter, the Clinton people concluded that it was serious and a basis for negotiation.

Under the Agreed Framework North Korea would freeze and eventually dismantle its nuclear weapons program. It would remain a party to the NPT, and once certain conditions of the agreement had been fulfilled, would allow inspections by the IAEA of sites not covered by the freeze.

The American team, led by Ambassador Gallucci, agreed that the parties would move toward "full normalization of political and economic relations."[12] The United States would provide formal assurances to North Korea against the threat or use of nuclear weapons. The parties would also reduce barriers to trade and investment, including restrictions on financial transactions. Each side would open a liaison office in the other's capital. The United States would provide two new light-water reactors for generating nuclear power; these would offset the energy lost by the freeze on other North Korean facilities. The United States would also furnish heavy fuel as another offset.

A week after the agreement was signed, the off-year elections in the United States gave the Republican party control of Congress. Some of the party's hard-liners immediately denounced the agreement with North Korea as appeasement. The administration was intimidated and thrown off balance, even though it had a strong case. The Agreed Framework halted a program that had already produced enough plutonium for five or six bombs and would become capable of annually reprocessing enough to make thirty more of them. Without the agreement, this forbidden program could have been expanded.

The six years that bracketed the signing of the Agreed Framework and the end of the Clinton era might be described as the halcyon time in relations between the United States and North Korea. That it was, but only when compared to any other moment in the relationship. A politically driven over-caution caused the administration to shrink from implementing the agreement.

Construction of the first replacement reactor was slow to begin. Delivery of the heavy fuel oil was sometimes delayed. Washington was moving, but slowly enough to accommodate the President's reelection strategy. Also, by 1996, Clinton may have believed reports that rampant food shortages would cause North Korea to collapse, thereby removing any need to fulfill the agreement. In February 1997, Pyongyang started warning that it would no longer be bound by the agreement if Washington didn't live up to its terms.[13]

Starting then, North Korea began edging back to the brink. First it took steps that seemed to foreshadow a resumption of plutonium reprocessing. That did not happen. At about this time, however, U.S. intelligence agencies were seeing scattered reports of movement by North Korea toward a uranium enrichment program. Pakistan, strapped for cash, offered, in effect, to swap North Korean help with its missile program for uranium enrichment technology based on a cascade of gas centrifuges.

The Clinton people didn't raise this matter with North Korea, mainly because the information was vague and uncertain. Also, the intelligence community was opposed to contacting the other side at that early stage; it wanted to learn more first. Although opinion was shifting by 2000, the administration judged that settling the uranium enrichment issue would require additional leverage that could be obtained only by building up the negotiating process.

An obvious question was why would the regime in Pyongyang risk ruining the recently improved and more stable relationship with the country that mattered most. A composite opinion of American specialists—former diplomats and currently serving and former officials from the intelligence community— runs like this:

- Kim Jong Il wanted some insurance in case the benefits from the Agreed Framework didn't materialize. Washington seemed to be dragging its feet on moving toward normalization of political relations, and Kim was resuming the only game he knew—tit for tat.
- In any case, when dealing with the Americans, North Koreans feel as if they can't have too many chips on the table. Military programs and the one-million-man army are their only leverage. They have no economy, no allies. They were looking for some edge, hence the highly enriched uranium (HEU) program.
- If the relationship with Washington went downhill, enriched uranium could become another cash crop.
- The military bureaucracy liked Pakistan's offer and recommended accepting it for security reasons. Kim Jong Il bought the recommendation.

Not much is known about what goes on within North Korea's bureaucratic structure; but American officials have heard about sharply contesting bodies of opinion from defectors, some diplomats, and knowledgeable South Koreans. There are hard-liners who see any negotiations with the United States as compromising security. And there are pragmatists who call themselves realists and think that, like it or not, they must deal with the United States; that it's possible to deal with the Americans and keep what North Korea needs for security. The "realists" see compromises as essential.

The tit for tat shifted into another arena—ballistic missiles. In 1996, talks between Washington and Pyongyang about curbing the latter's traffic in these weapons started, but over the next two years the U.S. side scheduled only two rounds of talks. The North Koreans, who wanted to make another deal with the United States, pressed the matter. In mid-June 1998, they went public with an offer to negotiate an end to both sales and development of ballistic missiles. But attached to the offer was a threat to resume tests if negotiations weren't held.[14]

The Clinton administration didn't take up the offer, and North Korea did carry out its threat by launching a three-stage rocket—the Taepodong I—on August 31, 1996. The missile's third stage malfunctioned, and it failed to put the satellite payload in orbit. Also, in conducting the test, North Korea had neither telemetry nor downrange ships. So there was no way of knowing whether the reentry vehicle survived the experience. But the missile's second stage passed over Japan and landed in the Pacific, 1,022 miles from the launch site. And the third stage was a solid-fueled rocket that North Korea had not been known to possess. For Japan, it was a shocking event, and the absence of a tougher response from the White House led

Japan to worry that Washington was downgrading its commitment to East Asia.

Congress issued a clarion call for building a defense against North Korean missile systems. But the administration had more to think about. The test occurred two weeks after the *New York Times* reported that U.S. intelligence had detected what appeared to be a secret North Korean underground nuclear weapons complex.[15]

Washington had to think carefully about what to do, although the only response that made sense was arranging another and more serious round of negotiations. Further efforts to contain and isolate North Korea would have been seen there as aggressive acts; a paranoid regime would have been left feeling victimized not by its own bad conduct but by the cruel devices of the world beyond.

Clinton's people knew from experience that negotiation was the only good option. But feelings about North Korea were running high, and Clinton needed a universally respected and experienced figure to manage the process. He persuaded a reluctant William Perry to become the North Korea policy coordinator.

Perry began by consulting Japan and South Korea. He then traveled to North Korea and proposed a sweeping trade: normal diplomatic relations with the United States, a peace treaty ending the Korean War, and improved relations with South Korea and Japan; in return, North Korea would be expected to reconfirm the stand-down of its nuclear programs and put an end to long-range missile development. The alternative, Perry indicated, would be a standoff, meaning that if Pyongyang stayed on course, America and its allies would take steps to protect themselves and isolate North Korea.[16]

Some good news, although slow to develop, began to appear. Kim Jong Il emerged from the shadow of his father and began to gather strength as leader. The scanty intelligence suggested an unattractive character—an indolent and bibulous womanizer, in most ways unlike his father. But like his father, Kim took charge and attached himself to a few capable and moderate figures, one of whom, Kang Sok Ju, a senior diplomat, had negotiated the Agreed Framework and served as Kim Il Sung's chief diplomatic advisor. Predictably, Kang was Perry's interlocutor in Pyongyang.

In South Korea, Kim Dae Jung, a deeply respected and legendary figure, was elected president early in 1998 and lost no time in making clear his intention to engage the North and improve relations. For decades, he had pressed for doing just that. Kim Dae Jung called his program the "Sunshine Policy." And besides speaking in positive terms about Kim Il Sung, he was contemplating the unprecedented summit conference they held in Pyongyang two years later.

In Pyongyang, Perry observed clear divisions within the regime. Before leaving, he suggested that if his proposals were too broad to be dealt with at once, North Korea could consider beginning with a small step, such as imposing a moratorium on further flight tests of its missiles. In turn, Washington would ease some economic sanctions. A month later, in mid-September 1999, North Korea agreed to the moratorium while talks with Washington continued. And Clinton then lifted sanctions that had banned most of the commercial traffic between the two countries.[17]

The meeting between the leaders of North and South Korea was scheduled for early June 2000. First, however, Kim Dae Jung felt a need to know something about the mysterious Kim Jong Il's agenda and his nature. His closest advisor, Lim Dong Won, flew secretly to Pyongyang on May 29 and met for four hours with Kim Jong Il. He returned to Seoul with an upbeat six-point report that seemed to belie the intelligence:

- He is a strong dictator, stronger than his father [whom Lim had met twice in the early 1990s].

- He is the only person who is open-minded and pragmatic in the North Korean system.
- He is a good listener. He took notes on the meeting . . . like a good student with a professor.
- When he is persuaded to another's point of view, he is decisive.
- He is gentle and polite to older people around him.
- He has a sense of humor.[18]

Although some sensitive issues, both national and international, produced a few tricky moments, the meeting went a good deal better than expected. And that, according to Kim Dae Jung, "was due in large measure to [Kim Jong Il's] ability to be receptive to new ideas and a willingness to change his views. . . . He didn't appear to be a cold-minded theoretician, but a very sensitive personality who had a sharp mind."[19]

"Kim Jong Il spent fifteen years in training for this job," says a former State Department official with long experience in Korean affairs. "He was the crown prince and has a few of the personality quirks that crown princes often have. But he is serious and smart as hell." He also has a reckless streak, according to equally experienced officials—American and South Korean—and unlike his father, the "Great Leader," he has something to prove.

Leon Sigal, an authority on the two Koreas, said of the summit meetings, "The South and the North pledged to reconcile, an irreversible step toward ending a half century of internecine conflict. By reaching accommodation, the onetime foes would be realigning relations in all of Northeast Asia and opening the way to regional cooperation on security."[20] Clinton responded at once by fulfilling his promise to end sanctions under the Trading with the Enemy Act.

Three months after the meeting, Kim Dae Jung told some American friends and Korean specialists that in his opinion Kim Jong Il had wanted to use the meeting to help generate desperately needed external assistance. Kim Dae Jung also suggested a growing trust in Pyongyang and that the South's policy was now aimed at assisting the North rather than undermining it. By the end of the year, the two Koreas had held four rounds of ministerial talks authorizing a wide range of cooperative ventures.[21]

In early October, North Korea renounced terrorism and joined the United States in a statement that "underscored their commitment to support the international legal regime combating international terrorism and to cooperate with each other in taking effective measures to fight terrorism." And they agreed to "exchange information regarding international terrorism."[22]

This was progress to which Kim Jong Il responded three days later by sending his second in command, Vice Marshal Jo Myong Rok, to the United States. A surprised Washington had been expecting to see an emissary but not the country's second most important person. Kim Jong Il was signaling that the time had come for serious movement on basic security issues. A joint communiqué issued on October 12 read, "Neither government would have hostile intent toward the other."[23] Here, it seemed, was the guarantee Pyongyang had been pursuing.

The second and great surprise was when Vice Marshal Jo met with Clinton and invited him to visit Pyongyang and work out differences between the countries in talks with the leader himself. Clinton couldn't do that, he explained, without preparing carefully, in part by arranging agreement on some preliminary steps. He proposed accomplishing that by sending then Secretary of State Madeleine Albright to Pyongyang, and he expressed hope that her visit would allow him to follow prior to his departure from office in three months' time.[24]

Albright arrived in Pyongyang just eleven days after the vice marshal's Washington visit. In her meetings with Kim Jong Il, he was accompanied only by Kang and an interpreter.

Albright presented a list of questions about North Korea's missile program that her entourage had given to North Korean experts several hours earlier. She apparently told Kim that some of the questions were technical and might require study. But Kim, she reported, picked up the list and immediately provided answers one by one without help or further study. Albright called it a "quite stunning" feat.[25]

Major progress was made. Kim offered to ban future production and deployment of all missiles with a range of 300 miles or more. These were the systems of greatest concern— the Nodong, the Taepodong I, and its successor, the Taepodong II, which was alleged to have an international capacity and had set off the pressure in Washington for a national missile defense. He also offered to halt the sale of missiles, missile components, technology, and training. That pledge would have banned systems that North Korea had already contracted to sell to other Third World countries.[26]

Since the range of his rockets would be limited, Kim Jong Il wanted assurance that North Korea's scientific satellites could be sent into outer space. The U.S. side offered to arrange for the launch of two to three satellites annually. Still, the freeze had to be made a verifiable ban; issues that remained to be settled included the elimination of North Korean missiles and on-site monitoring to verify the cessation of missile production and deployment. The Americans also wanted to extend the freeze to missile systems capable of ranges exceeding 180 miles.[27]

Kim Jong Il told Albright that he agreed to the need for verification of compliance, but he could not accept "intrusive verification" because his country was neither an outlaw state nor a defendant in a trial.[28] Clearly, more work lay ahead. But so did what for the North Koreans would be the main event— Clinton's visit. Their intention may have been to make their major concessions and tie together the loose ends when he came. But he didn't. Only Clinton can say why. There may have been too many loose ends that needed clearing up prior to a visit. The presidential election on November 7 dragged on for another five weeks, leaving hard feelings in its wake. Some said the President shouldn't travel abroad if the country was facing a constitutional crisis. And the violence between Israelis and Palestinians that Clinton had tried to head off had nonetheless erupted.

With the prospect of Clinton's visit ebbing, negotiations between Washington and Pyongyang led nowhere. On January 17, 2002, the ex-president said as much to the Council on Foreign Relations. "We were very close," he said, "to ending the North Korean missile program in the year 2001. I believe if I had been willing to go there, we would have ended it."[29]

The Korean crisis that began to boil up a year or so after 9/11 was widely judged, especially by the Bush administration, to have been caused by Pyongyang's flagrant violation of international agreements. And there is something to that. Others would argue that in larger measure the crisis was created by Bush's determination to ignore and/or reject the Clinton administration's engagement with North Korea and its support for South Korea's Sunshine Policy. The absence of policy is policy, heavy-handed at that.

Shortly before the November 2000 elections, a North Korean party newspaper, *Nodong Sinmun*, said that the regime was prepared to work with whichever candidate won. Pyongyang then sent very positive signals to the new administration. In February 2001, North Korea's Permanent Representative to the UN, Lee Hyong Choi, went to Washington to convey the regime's eagerness to resume the negotiating process. This gesture surprised the State Department's Asia watchers; they had expected the North Koreans to step back and do some posturing before agreeing to engage the new administration.

But then, on March 6, just six weeks after taking office, the administration started up the path that led to nowhere in its relations with the two Koreas. Kim Dae Jung, the winner of the previous year's Nobel Peace Prize, met that day with Bush. Kim had hoped to acquire support for reconciliation with the North. He failed, as Bush made painfully clear, when they appeared together in a televised news conference.

Just the day before, Colin Powell had spoken in positive terms about what had gone before. "As I said previously," he began, "and especially in my confirmation hearings, we do plan to engage with North Korea to pick up where President Clinton and his administration left off."

Powell was required to eat his words the next day, just minutes before Bush and Kim Dae Jung made their brief appearance before the press. "The President forcefully made the point that we are undertaking a full review of our relationship with North Korea," he said. "There was some suggestion that imminent negotiations are about to begin—that is not the case."[30]

Besides publicly disdaining Kim Dae Jung's Sunshine Policy, Bush privately discouraged him from concluding a peace agreement with the North or providing it with electricity. Odder still, he disparaged Kim Jong Il, calling him a "pygmy" and telling a reporter he "loathed him."[31]

Talk of this kind against a leader who had recently offered to stop making and selling ballistic missiles was both puzzling and worrisome. Questions arose: Was the missile deal still on the table? If not, was Powell, too, a casualty? However, despite their occasional bluster and florid rhetoric, the North Koreans refused to accept rejection. Having come so far, and given the heavy U.S. self-interest in discouraging the spread of destructive weapons, they may have assumed that matters would find their way back on track. The administration had said there would be a policy review—normal procedure. After some posturing designed to save face, the North Koreans signaled their readiness to return to engagement when the review was out of the way.

But Bush equated talking to them with rewarding bad behavior. In March, the administration gave Pyongyang more to think about. The highlights of a nuclear posture review were leaked to the *Los Angeles Times*. It sounded threatening, especially the references to creating a new family of nuclear weapons to attack underground bunkers. North Korea is believed to have a network of deep underground tunnels second to none.

In June, Washington announced the end of the policy review and noted its intention to seek "improved implementation" of the 1994 Agreed Framework, reinterpreting it to require prompt nuclear inspections without offering anything in return and insisting that progress toward an agreement on missiles would depend on progress on other issues of concern. That language ruled out movement on any issue.[32] As seen from Pyongyang, Washington had just made two mistakes: (1) announcing the end of the review without *first* informing North Korea of its content; (2) failing to schedule talks to discuss implementing whatever steps the review might have recommended.

After the review, Washington's line on talks with Pyongyang became "any time, any place," but it was impossible to reach agreement within the administration's contentious parts on what to say to North Korea or when and where to say it. There was North Korea's pilot HEU project to consider; the Bush people had of course learned about it from the outgoing administration, but their internal struggles blocked movement on that issue as well. Bush, it seemed, wanted to do nothing about North Korea other than isolate it. What he should have done was authorize Powell to (1) begin serious talks on nuclear issues and (2) define reprocessing spent fuel as a red line.

Later in June, however, the Pyongyang regime conveyed a

message that was intended to resonate. "We do not regard the United States as a one-hundred-year enemy," a foreign ministry official told a visiting American academic delegation. "However Delphic the language, the North Koreans attached huge importance to it," says one of the State Department's experienced Korea hands. "That statement was used once before—by Kim Jong Il himself—and because it did come directly from him, it provided the pro-engagement advocates with cover and became the key to North Korea's overtures to Washington."

Pyongyang was also seeking a promise from the new administration that it would not attack North Korea. The request offered Washington an opportunity to reaffirm the No Hostile Intent declaration that was reached in October 2000 with Marshal Jo. The administration's refusal to do so was interpreted in Pyongyang, not surprisingly, as a repudiation of that agreement.

Around this time, the North Koreans were busily creating diplomatic ties with most members of the EU as well as a number of countries elsewhere. Pyongyang saw this campaign as worth pursuing both for its own sake and for the favorable impression it was intended to make on Washington. There was also the hope that expanding its horizon might help North Korea advance the day when normal diplomatic relations with Japan could be established.

The North Koreans expected the Bush administration to settle down, draw from the lessons of the past, and restart a conversation that would lead somewhere. But most of what they heard were complaints about their missiles and talk of the compelling need for a national missile defense to counter them. The North Koreans countercomplained that Bush's people were beating the drum without first talking to them. They reminded Washington that they had already said they had no problem with the Bush agenda, of which their missile program was item one. They said that agreements already reached with the previous administration covered issues involving both nuclear weapons and ballistic missiles. They were saying, Let's talk about these things. We've talked about them before. These topics are still on the table, subject to further negotiation. In fact, everything is on the table.

There ensued a good deal of finger-pointing by both sides. In late August 2001, North Korea entreated Washington not to undermine the foundation of what had been agreed to earlier. Their language reflected frustration but also worry. They referred to the joint communiqué of October 12, 2000, and again cited the American concern with North Korean missiles and suggested pointedly that preserving consistency in foreign policy was important even for the United States. Still trying to get Washington's attention, the regime also noted that the joint communiqué had cited a concern with terrorism and that an even earlier statement had encouraged international efforts to contain terrorism.

Other capitals were asking why Washington didn't just pocket the agreement worked out with North Korea by Clinton if the missiles represented a serious threat. And given the administration's strong feelings about nuclear proliferation, why not choke off the possibility that long-range North Korean missile systems might one day be mated with nuclear weapons? The accord on missiles had been part of a process that began with the Agreed Framework and, logically, would have led to further steps to limit the development, deployment, and sale of highly destructive weapons. Whether to take these steps jointly with North Korea, however gradually, was hardly a close question, as seen by other governments. For European leaders, it was a no-brainer. For North Korea's frankly worried neighbors, sustaining both the arms-control process and movement toward reconciling the two Koreas was vital.

Had they been made aware of what the Bush administration

learned in November 2001, their level of concern would have been higher. Intelligence analysts at the Lawrence Livermore National Laboratory reported then that North Korea had begun construction of a uranium enrichment plant. (The report was confirmed seven months later by a National Intelligence Estimate done by the CIA and other intelligence agencies.) The Livermore report also disclosed that Pakistan had provided the plans that showed how uranium is enriched.[33] For the next eleven months, the administration concealed the evidence of this illicit program from the American public and most other governments, probably because it wanted to avoid allowing anything to interfere with its design for Iraq.

The neighborhood's anxiety was nonetheless sharpened by Bush's "axis of evil" speech in January 2002. But on June 10, Powell set out a four-point agenda for talks with North Korea: These included ending sales of destructive weapons, eliminating its long-range missile programs, and coming into full compliance with IAEA safeguards. In reply, Pyongyang accepted Powell's agenda, suggesting a new or revised Agreed Framework to accommodate it.[34] The issue divided Rumsfeld and his people from Powell and his. Cheney sided with Rumsfeld, and so did national security advisor Condoleezza Rice. We cannot trust them or deal with them, said the hard-liners.

In late August 2002, Undersecretary John Bolton traveled to Seoul, where he called North Korea "an evil regime that is armed to the teeth, including with weapons of mass destruction. . . . President Bush's use of the term 'axis of evil' to describe Iran, Iraq, and North Korea was more than a rhetorical flourish—it was factually correct."[35] Bolton is a former protégé of Jesse Helms and a senior member of the hard-right faction within Bush's national security apparatus. Colin Powell is nominally his boss, but on most issues Bolton distances himself from Powell and works closely with kindred spirits in the White House and OSD.

Bolton's speech went down badly in Seoul, but Pyongyang yet again turned the other cheek, issuing a soft statement that had been used before: "If the U.S. has the will to drop its hostile policy toward the DPRK [Democratic Peoples Republic of Korea] it will have a dialogue with the U.S. to clear the U.S. of its worries over security."

In July, just before Bolton's visit, Kim Jong Il kicked his diplomacy into a higher gear, putting special emphasis on the regional players: Japan, China, South Korea, and Russia. "We saw frantic diplomatic efforts," recalls a former official from the intelligence community. "Kim Jong Il was meeting every Russian who came by." And he was edging in small steps toward normalizing relations with Japan.

In Japan, various figures, including Prime Minister Junichiro Koizumi, were aware of their country's need to come to terms with its past and begin to play a role within the region. Japan was a confused society. It had acquired a system of values built on a system of shared beliefs that developed during the Cold War. Later, the values gave way, with nothing to replace them other than a quest for material prosperity.

Koizumi also recognized North Korea's need to negotiate not just with America but also with Japan. On August 30, just one day after Bolton's visit to Seoul, Koizumi surprised the world by announcing that he and Kim Jong Il would hold the first ever meeting between heads of state of their two countries. When they met on September 17, Kim astonished both Koizumi and his country by apologizing for the abduction of twelve Japanese citizens, eight of whom had died. He also apologized for intrusions by North Korean warships into Japanese waters, disingenuously shifting the blame to reckless officers. Finally, he promised to extend indefinitely the moratorium on North Korean missile tests to which he had been committed until 2003.

In Washington at this time, Bush made public the new doctrine that seemed to substitute preventive war for deterrence. By then, it seemed that he wanted tension with rogue states at some level and little else.

But the surprise and the flurry of comment arising from the events of September were eclipsed by a seemingly more portentous event a few weeks later. After twenty-two months of avoiding contact with North Korea, the administration sent Assistant Secretary of State John Kelly for two days of talks (October 4–5) in Pyongyang. Washington had Kelly on a short leash. Even the customary dinner laid on by his hosts was cancelled prior to Kelly's arrival. His talking points amounted to an assertion that North Korea was embarked on an HEU program. Because Kelly didn't cite the evidence, although it existed, it was not an accusation as such, at least as seen by the other side's chief negotiator, the very same Kang Sok Ju who, as noted, had for many years operated as the leadership's good cop in dealings with Washington. Although Kang conceded nothing, neither did he deny the tacit charge that his government was engaged in what amounted to an illicit nuclear weapons program. He was probably getting on-the-spot guidance from Kim Jong Il.

What Kelly could have said but didn't was, Are you telling us that indeed you do have a uranium enrichment program? But he and his colleagues had been surprised and thrown off balance; they had expected a harder and more negative response from Kang. What Kelly did say, in effect, was that North Korea must do the right thing and dismantle its illegal programs. According to a North Korean version, Kelly said a failure to comply would mean no dialogue with the United States, and that relations between the two Koreas would be jeopardized.

But the administration continued to sit on the evidence and the implicit admission of wrongdoing by the North Koreans. Bush and his advisors were determined that nothing should interfere with their plans for Iraq. Congress was about to vote on Bush's war powers resolution. The Senate vote, which for a moment looked iffy, was scheduled for October 10, a week after Kelly's departure from Pyongyang.

But shortly after the Senate voted, news of the North Korean HEU program began to seep out. First, Barbara Slavin, a reporter for *USA Today* with very good sources, was writing a piece for publication on October 17. The administration pre-empted by calling various major news organizations so as not to be left behind, and to have time to spin the story. It caused serious concern. Kim Jong Il, in yet another trip to the confessional, had lifted the veil on an illegal program. But why?

Then the North Koreans went public. Without confirming or denying Kelly's assertion, their official news agency announced that North Korea would negotiate a settlement of the nuclear issue provided the United States recognized its sovereignty, offered a nonaggression guarantee, and didn't interfere with its economic development (meaning no imposition of sanctions). These were conditions already promised, said the North Koreans pointedly. They were contained in a U.S.–North Korea joint statement signed in New York on June 11, 1993, and reaffirmed in a later agreement, but an agreement that Pyongyang was now violating.

Washington reacted guardedly, at least at first. It wanted to settle the flare-up peacefully, partly because it was so distracted by Iraq. The word "crisis" was formally eschewed by Colin Powell. Also, Washington had to sample the reactions of China, Japan, South Korea, and Russia. No one wanted to see a fight on the Korean peninsula.

In mid-December, Powell assured North Korea that the United States had no intention of attacking. Then Pyongyang complicated matters by going back to the brink. First, it announced that it would restart work at three abandoned nuclear reactors. In late December, North Korea broke seals around a pool holding 8,000 of the spent fuel rods at their Yongbyon nuclear plant. The IAEA's two resident inspectors then left the country. A few weeks later, North Korea announced its intention to withdraw from the NPT. The IAEA inspectors, it said, would not be allowed to return.

In theory, the administration had three options: containment, war, and negotiation. Containment wasn't a good option, because it would mean accepting a development that wasn't really acceptable. North Korea would be left free to build nuclear weapons and, worse yet, to sell the technology to anyone who was buying. Still, some members of the administration did for a time consider what they called tailored containment. It would have amounted to isolating North Korea economically by asking its neighbors to cut economic ties and urging the UN to impose sanctions. The United States would order its forces to intercept the missile exports that Pyongyang was relying on for income. However, by proposing UN sanctions or sanctions of its own, the United States would have crossed one of North Korea's red lines; Pyongyang had often warned that any such move would be regarded as an act of war. Colin Powell swiftly intervened to make sure that Washington did not seek UN sanctions and that tailored containment came to nothing.

Although the military option had few takers (least of all among the uniformed military), they were in key places, notably the vice president's office and OSD. North Korea had altered its strategy from one based on seizure of territory to one of holding Seoul hostage with long-range artillery tubes deployed just above the Demilitarized Zone (DMZ). Another conflict, in the military's view, would mean the deaths of hundreds of thousands of South Koreans, thousands of American troops, and destruction throughout much of North Korea. The first few days would likely produce devastation on a scale not seen since the battle for Stalingrad. Powell said on December 29, 2002, that the United States had no immediate plans to attack North Korea and force it to abandon its nuclear program. "We have months to watch this unfold, see what happens," he said. Rumsfeld had warned a week earlier that the United States could fight two wars at the same time—against Iraq and North Korea.[36]

Negotiation seemed to be the only viable option, even if all parties, except for Powell and his deputy, Richard Armitage, who was the hands-on manager of the problem, were ruling out negotiation with a rogue state that broke solemn international obligations. Face had also become a large issue for Washington, as it never ceases being for Pyongyang.

The administration's rarely uttered but well-known objection to direct negotiation lay in its charge that Clinton's Agreed Framework had allowed the nuclear problem to fester. Powell felt differently and said so in January. "The previous administration I give great credit to for freezing the plutonium site. Lots of nuclear weapons were not made because of the Agreed Framework and the work of President Clinton and his team."[37]

But then the situation abruptly went from serious to critical. In late February, North Korea restarted a nuclear reactor it had mothballed as part of the original Agreed Framework. The plant was judged capable of producing enough fissile material to make one nuclear weapon per year.[38] Worse yet, spy satellite intelligence indicated that a larger plant would probably be reactivated, possibly within a few weeks, at which point the 8,000 spent fuel rods could be reprocessed into weapons-grade plutonium. Once the reprocessing began, North Korea would be able to produce one bomb a month, according to estimates.

Senior figures from past administrations, including Brent Scowcroft and William Perry, were urging the White House to do what it had steadfastly refused to do: negotiate one-on-one with the North Koreans. For weeks, China, Japan, South

Korea, and Russia had argued for doing exactly that. And according to a remarkably revealing article in the *New York Times*, various ex-officials were making this case to Condoleezza Rice. The article went on to note that earlier in February, Armitage had

> used his testimony in Congress to try to expand that strategy, and that his efforts left Mr. Bush "off the wall angry," said a senior administration official, whose account was corroborated by several White House officials. . . .
>
> Mr. Armitage praised President Bill Clinton's 1994 deal with North Korea for preventing earlier bomb making by the north. [His] testimony led to a meeting at the White House at which Mr. Bush directed Secretary of State Colin L. Powell and other officials to ban all public discussion of one-on-one talks with the North. . . . "We're at the point," said one official involved in the internal debate, "where nothing is happening and no one knows how we will respond when the bomb making starts."[39]

Attitudes of depressing predictability had led to the impasse. Unless the North Koreans agreed first to dismantle their nuclear programs verifiably, the administration wouldn't talk to them. But the North Koreans would do nothing under threat or pressure. Bush wanted to use neighboring countries and/or the Security Council to bring heavy pressure on Pyongyang. The other governments, although aware that North Korea's neighbors would have to be involved at some stage, judged the U.S. push for multilateral talks as designed to avoid actual negotiations with North Korea. Washington, some of them warned, could not just sit there and wait for North Korea to bow to pressure or undergo a regime change. Neither would happen. And if Washington stuck to its position, the others worried that South Korea might even react by dissolving its alliance with the United States. Japan's reaction was unlikely to go that far, but might nonetheless be very negative. In Tokyo, the nuclear issue had become real and immediate, and America's so-called nuclear shield didn't seem altogether credible. A decision by Japan to acquire nuclear weapons of its own couldn't be ruled out and, if taken, would be judged, quite simply, as catastrophic. China and Russia, although deeply worried, were reluctant to lean heavily on a client state, especially at Washington's behest, although China did begin to put pressure on Pyongyang in the spring of 2003.

The related but still more serious question was what the administration would do if North Korea crossed the Rubicon by reprocessing spent fuel. Would Washington strike at the Yongbyon facility preemptively? And if North Korea responded by attacking the South, how would Washington react? It seemed to other governments that events might outpace efforts to manage them, in which case no contingency, however dire, could be ruled out.

On the eve of the war with Iraq, the administration warned North Korea not to take advantage of the situation by making a provocative move. (This kind of warning is called "foaming the runway" by diplomats.) The response was described as "sullen and noncommittal." But among the most worrisome contingencies on many minds was the prospect of India and Pakistan shooting their way to the head of an agenda dominated by Iraq and the Korean peninsula.

Armitage, in testimony before the Senate Committee on Foreign Relations, said the United States feared North Korea would seek to stave off economic collapse by selling fissile material to rogue states or terrorist organizations. Within several months, he said, North Korea could extract 25 to 30 kilograms of plutonium—enough for four to six nuclear weapons—from the 8,000 fuel rods stored at Yongbyon.[40]

Ten days after this testimony, Brent Scowcroft and Daniel Poneman, who had worked with Armitage on the National Security Council staff, sounded the same warning: "If North Korea continues to view unconventional weapons exports as its chief cash crop, it will find numerous customers with adequate means and motive. Access to plutonium could shave years off the efforts of al-Qaeda and other terrorists to obtain the weapon of ultimate destruction."[41]

Two weeks earlier, CIA Director George Tenet had told the House Armed Services Committee that Kim Jong Il was seeking political leverage from his nuclear programs. "He is trying to negotiate a fundamentally different relationship with us," Tenet said, "one that implicitly tolerates nuclear weapons programs. [He] is committed to retaining and enlarging his nuclear stockpile."[42]

On background, a senior official from another intelligence agency made the point differently. "The North Koreans read the tea leaves," he said, "and see that their current tactic isn't working." (He meant going to the brink in order to get what they need from Washington.) "So they won't roll over and dismantle their nuclear programs verifiably, not completely anyway but maybe partially. They will leave some uncertainty because, besides not trusting us, they distrust their neighbors and will want to leave everyone in some doubt as to what they actually have."

Still another senior official, also speaking privately, said, "At the end of this, he [Kim Jong Il] may get one of two things he doesn't have now: a good-sized nuclear arsenal, like Pakistan's, or direct talks with the United States."[43] No one in or out of the intelligence community, or any part of the government, could claim with confidence to know how Kim Jong Il would play his hand. Some officials worried aloud about a slippery slope to war with North Korea. That probably won't happen. Nonetheless, some experienced people think it may be too late to stop North Korea's HEU program, at least verifiably, if only because all or most of it can remain hidden. After Iraq, the argument goes, the North Koreans probably feel a need to have a deterrent, or at least pretend to have one. Creative ambiguity is the effect they may wish to achieve. But the plutonium program is different. That probably could be stopped through negotiation because it could otherwise be stopped militarily; it lies unconcealed and in the open.

Among the few things that can be said with confidence about the North Koreans are these:

- In 1994, Kim Jong Il gave up a huge plutonium program—one that was larger than the programs of Israel, India, and Pakistan combined; it would have provided enough fissile material for the production of thirty nuclear weapons per year. Now he has an HEU program that is still embryonic but could get much bigger.
- North Korea sold medium-range ballistic missiles to Iran and Pakistan, a transaction that no other supplier would have made but one that got Washington's full attention.

Experience shows that the menace presented by the North Koreans should be manageable—at least compared to other situations such as Pakistan or even Iran, with authority there unevenly divided between the reformist government and the hard-line clergy. North Korea has had no involvement with terrorism. And in 2000 Kim Jong Il offered to stop producing and deploying the missile systems of concern—the ones that could travel more than 300 miles. Moreover, he said he would no longer sell missiles and related technologies. That offer may still be there, waiting to be picked up.

The question arose: Would Kim Jong Il be willing to sell off his HEU program for the political and security assurances that in the past dominated his agenda? More exactly, would he, in return for those assurances, be willing to dismantle the program verifiably? And would he agree to shun the lucrative export market for fissile material and related components? Many experienced Korea watchers tend to feel, if a little shakily, that he probably would. But, they would add, we won't know unless and until serious negotiations are allowed to go forward.

There are both similarities and serious differences between the crisis with North Korea that Clinton's team faced and the one that has emerged more recently. In both cases, the other countries in the region were and are closely involved. And U.S. goals haven't changed. North Korea's behavior has remained much the same, but is harder to read, and Kim Jong II is less predictable than his father. The more important difference is North Korea's HEU program, another vector of threat and an easier path to nuclear weapons. Washington must draw a strong red line and stop this program. The administration urgently needs to develop a road map leading toward a nuclear-free and stable Korean peninsula. The road map must be credible, meaning that it must be seen as a basis for negotiation by North Korea and also by its neighbors.

The Bush administration, unlike its predecessor, has played for time as if time were on the U.S. side. It isn't.

Chapter 5

Ties That Bind?

The decade between the collapse of the Soviet Union and September 11, 2001, was a parenthesis. The events of that day pushed history into a new current. Nowhere was the redirection as pronounced as in relations between America and Russia. Together, it seemed, they might exercise the principal influence on global security arrangements and perhaps global stability in the years directly ahead.

Vladimir Putin, Russia's president, grasped at once the meaning of 9/11. More rapidly than his peers, with the possible exception of Britain's leader, Tony Blair, he saw the event as allowing Russia, even a much diminished Russia, to align itself with the United States in a campaign against the threat from terrorism that impartially confronted them both. In effect, Washington's new first priority was converging with Putin's— Putin had run for election as president on an anti-terrorism platform.

Putin's broad purpose—to link his ailing, self-absorbed country to the United States while moving it into the European mainstream—had been gathering force for some time. "He arrived in power with the most pronounced pro-Western policy bias of any politician in Russian history," Sergei Markov, director of the Institute for Political Studies in Moscow, has said. More exactly, Putin aspired to an arrangement in which America would increasingly share world leadership with Russia, a potentially great power that is currently power-lite, has vital interests in both Europe and Asia, and can influence events in both regions.

September 11 reminded all sides that momentous events create the impetus for momentous change. Still, two and only two capitals—Washington and Moscow—were in a position to turn what occurred then to serious advantage. Doing so, however, would require each to find a stable balance between its own interests and those of the other.

Although Washington and Moscow do share some high-priority interests, they also have important differences. Russia, as noted, wants to continue earning large sums of money by marketing nuclear technology to Iran—a commerce to which Washington strongly objects. Strategic differences also exist. The administration of President George W. Bush favors missile defense over deterrence, whereas Russians continue to see mutual deterrence as the sole purpose of the nuclear forces deployed by the two countries.

Bush wanted to connect with Putin, not least to have access to Russia's human intelligence–gathering resources in Iraq; these far exceeded America's limited capabilities. Whether Putin supported the U.S. approach to Iraq was going to depend on the price Bush was willing to pay. As early as December 2001, Putin cautioned the United States against extending the war to Iraq after the campaign in Afghanistan was concluded.

The Iraq issue put trade, oil, and geopolitics on the table. Russia has had large commercial interests in Iraq, including a $40 billion trade arrangement reached late in 2001. Putin wanted to protect that arrangement and to be able to sell goods to Iraq that Russia can't sell anywhere else. Oil was the most elusive piece of the package. Putin had insisted on a Russian share of Iraq's oil, the world's second-largest reserve. As many as 300 Russian companies were doing business with Iraq, under a UN program that allowed Iraqis to sell oil to pay for food and medicine. Russian firms controlled the rights to sell 40 percent of Iraq's oil on world markets.[1] Iraqi commitments to these companies, if realized, would have amounted to hundreds and perhaps billions of dollars.[2]

Putin may have seen Iraq as a win-win situation for him, whatever Bush did. A U.S. invasion might very well have caused his stock at home to go up, since he had on occasion, including the run-up to the war, made clear that he did not support regime change. And if in the end the United States did not invade, Putin could have been perceived as having had a role in preventing it.

Putin's role in helping with the North Korean problem was more apparent than real. He alone among the key players had developed a rapport with Kim Jong Il. China had more leverage with the North Korean regime than Russia, but was less disposed to use it. And Russia is more trusted in Pyongyang than China. However, even though Kim Jong Il has tended to accept any help he can get, he has insisted on settling issues affecting the security of his realm with Washington.

What would become of Putin's efforts to steer a westward course was likely to depend on whether he could prevail against the all but pervasive resistance to the move within his national security bureaucracy. Unlike his predecessor, Boris Yeltsin, he can count on a degree of support and credibility at home that allows him to make deals. And because he was not complicit in the dissolution of the Soviet Union, he is perceived by Russians to have a stronger connection to their interests. By having succeeded in consolidating presidential power, Putin has had more running room than Yeltsin had and can maneuver against the grain. And he is doing just that—taking on, and dominating, for the moment the larger part of Russia's political elite, which sees anti-Americanism as the right strategic direction.

In that light, a few of Bush's aides began to see Putin as someone who could make deals that stuck. This view was a major departure from the sharply negative line on Russia they began with, a time when the status of Russia policy was consciously downgraded and Bush's national security advisor, Condoleezza Rice, could suggest in a newspaper interview that Russia was still regarded as a threat.

Putin is seeking what could be called parity of esteem for his troubled country, but for much of Russia's foreign-policy establishment, the anti-American chord still resonates. A comment one hears in Moscow is that after the Cold War there was no money to be made in Washington fighting Russia, whereas Russians can still make a decent living fighting the United States. Anything good for America, they think, must be bad for Russia.

The war against Serbia created a strong wave of anti-Western, anti-NATO, and, above all, anti-American sentiment in Russia. NATO enlargement, like most such issues, was a topic discussed mainly within elite circles, but it, too, became a popular issue after NATO intervened in the Kosovo conflict.

Russians tended to see the first round of NATO enlargement as an example of the West taking advantage of Russian weakness and, as Dimitri Trenin has said, "redrawing the lines" that divided Europe. "The bulk of the Russian establishment (still) resents what some refer to as NATO's eastern march, because it eats away at their self-esteem and the traditional notion of Russia as a great power."[3]

Putin was under pressure to fix Russia's economy, but he wasn't under pressure from anywhere to forge a Western connection. So he began, in effect, surrendering long-standing

Russian strategic positions and thereby more or less isolating himself from Moscow's power ministries. Most Russians deplore the new round of NATO enlargement, which they see as bringing the Western alliance into space they once controlled. But Putin didn't challenge the proposed expansion to Russian borders, even though his minister of defense, Sergey Ivanov, and other senior officials have remained openly hostile to the move. And he quietly accepted cancellation of the ABM Treaty.

These and other concessions that appear to collide with Russian interests are judged by various Bush advisors as not affecting Putin. They think Putin can handle any flare-up from them. They could be wrong. The withdrawal from the treaty was seen at the time as a massive snub of Putin, even if unintended, especially since it served no immediate purpose. Much or most of the development and testing of components involved in the national missile defense program could be done over a period of several years without violating the ABM Treaty. Also, Putin was willing to amend the treaty in ways that would have increased Washington's comfort level by making the agreement more relevant to the altered environment.

Putin has positioned himself as the reasonable partner who takes an international approach to arms control and other strategic issues. And in trying to become part of the Western system, he has swallowed a lot. In the years ahead, he may trump his legion of critics in Moscow, but only if he gets a big return on his political investment in the West.

His behavior is replete with contradictions. He is trying to create more independent courts and strengthen the rule of law. Unlike Yeltsin, Putin gets along with the Duma and seems to respect the legislative process. But he has interfered in local elections, and he is hypersensitive to criticism. Noting that Yeltsin's tolerance of powerful and corrupt personalities harmed him as much as anything, Putin worked hard to distance himself from the "oligarchs" and from any hint of corruption.

After Yeltsin, Russians liked the idea of a president who came to work every day. The first book about Putin was called *The German in the Kremlin.* His use of four-letter words in news conferences has also played well and seemed to establish him as a real guy. Unlike Yeltsin, Putin doesn't get drunk or fall into rivers. For many of his citizens, Yeltsin's unleaderlike behavior seemed rather endearingly Russian. But most Russians prefer the man with the black belt in judo who exudes a quiet authority and has shown that he can hold his own at the top table. They see him as part of the solution to various problems, not a problem himself.

Paradoxically, support for Putin's major policies has remained low. The power ministries and opinionmakers will continue to feel that he is maneuvering against their country's larger interests. There appears to be no good or easy exit from the war in Chechnya. Grigory Yavlinsky, leader of the reform party, Yabloko, says, "Anyone who predicts what will happen in Russia is an idiot."[4]

Still, Putin did have to worry about the effect of a move against Iraq on regional stability, not least the risk that if the United States went after Iraq, Iran might in one way or another be next. He had to reckon with a large body of Russian opinion that saw the United States as running amok. He could not be viewed as approving the use of force by the United States against Russian interests. These interests are heavily engaged in Iran.

In aspiring to a role for Russia that accords with its potential reach and impact on world affairs, Putin has relied on support from key West European governments, notably Britain and Germany. He had hoped and probably expected them to exercise a moderating influence on Washington.

Putin usually plays black, preferring to let other key players make the opening moves. But that changed in the feverish post-9/11 days. He was the first leader to call Bush after the attacks. He approved the use of bases in Uzbekistan and else-where in Central Asia for strikes against the Taliban. Next, he visited Germany's chancellor, Gerhard Schroeder, in Berlin and wowed the Bundestag with a speech delivered in fluent German and studded with quotes from Goethe and Schiller. Russia was segueing into Europe.

But Putin's role model, quite clearly, was Tony Blair, if only because he, too, grasped the significance of September 11 and, more important, because he has sustained Britain's privileged relationship with the United States. The special quality of that relationship is what Putin seeks to acquire for Russia. He is not tempted to play off any of the Europeans against the United States. He wants to be influential in Europe by using Blair and to strengthen Russia's new relationship with NATO.

Blair gives a triangular aspect to the Bush-Putin relation-ship to the extent that he succeeds in anchoring himself to each of them. Blair and Putin were en rapport even before 9/11. Blair was the first leader to visit Putin in St. Petersburg before he took office as president. But their link tightened, mainly because they think alike about how best to sustain the anti-terrorist coalition and how to reconfigure the security system. Connecting Russia to the Western security apparatus—NATO at twenty, as it became known—was a top-down Blair initia-tive. Moreover, neither's position on missile defense is close to Bush's. On that and other strategic issues, they are similar to each other.

Although the relationship between the United States and Britain is famously special, it's not so special that it can't be shaken from time to time. After 9/11, it was shaken in Afghanistan and beyond. Bush made promises to Blair that he then reneged on under pressure from the Pentagon. Like Putin, Tony Blair has yielded to Bush on the most sensitive strategic issues, along with further enlargement of NATO, a step that Whitehall deplored with an intensity that nearly matched that of Putin's people. The British and various other NATO members worried that two rounds of enlargement, both of them born of American pressure, would make the structure larger, looser, and less relevant; the focus of security concerns is likely to be terrorism and proliferating weapons of mass destruction—issues that NATO is not well equipped to deal with. Finally, the British and Russians share a feeling that despite having provided a lot of support—moral and political— they have realized little or nothing in return, apart from the credit for having been solidly steadfast from 9/11 on.

Well before September 11, a few European leaders, starting with Blair, concluded that Western and Russian strategic interests were becoming alike and that collective security arrangements that lacked Russian participation no longer made sense. Indeed, Blair wanted to see Russia become a de facto member of NATO. And immediately after 9/11, without checking with Bush, he apparently "stunned" Putin by offering to arrange Russia's passage into the NATO sanctum. In return, Putin would allow the United States to fly its bombers over Central Asian states that remained within Russia's sphere of influence.[5] Blair sold this thinking to Bush during their meeting in Crawford, Texas, in November 2001.

But Blair and his officials then had to wage a seesaw battle with some of Bush's advisors, even though the President himself had approved the essentials of London's position. "What was agreed to at Crawford was left to fend for itself in the bureaucratic jungle dominated by OSD [Office of the Secretary of Defense]," said a senior State Department official. The outcome was left in doubt for months. For a time, it appeared as if Donald Rumsfeld had succeeded in undoing the deal his boss had just made. Colin Powell supported Blair and, as on so many issues, clashed with Rumsfeld, who drew support from most of the other senior people who had the President's ear.

In the end, a watered-down version of Blair's proposal was adopted, and the new NATO-Russia Council was launched officially in Rome on May 28, 2002. Putin may envisage its modest arrangements one day fulfilling a two-generation-long Russian dream of a pan-European security system, in which Russia would deploy the largest military force and be able to block any alliance military action of which it disapproved. That would play very well at home, as would steps aimed at fulfilling Putin's loftiest goals—embedding Russia in Europe and the world economy.

Blair has labored to reconcile his European credentials and determination to be a leader of the EU with his strenuous interest in sustaining a privileged relationship with Washington. On various issues, especially Iraq, the chattering classes at home and in various capitals have accused him of being overly submissive to Bush. Blair obviously doesn't agree. He has appeared confident that whatever attitudes they strike, European leaders take comfort from his closeness to Washington. They think it's very useful for at least one European to have a voice that may be heard. As to whether other Europeans see Blair as one of them, he believes they do. The special relationship, he feels, gives Britain influence in Europe it would not otherwise have.

From the start, Blair wanted his European colleagues to regard Bush as a strong and useful president. Returning to London from his first meeting with Bush, he called in a senior aide, John Sawers, and instructed him to summon all the EU ambassadors to London. As instructed, Sawers gave these diplomats a very upbeat assessment of Bush. Some of them concluded that Blair saw Bush as someone who could lead the charge with himself supplying the moral imperative. Their governments, however, were not persuaded.

Blair has a Gladstonian sense of Britain cast in the role of a force for good. And like Bush, he does identify evil and is concerned with doing something about ridding the world of evil-doers. An example was his decision to intervene in Sierra Leone in 2000, despite the uneasiness of his military advisors. He and they would have been more comfortable if Britain's EU partners had been willing to help. Each of them was asked to contribute something—a battalion, equipment, whatever. They all said no, including France and Germany, the first two asked. Only Poland, although not yet a member of the EU, volunteered a small force. This incident could hardly have weakened Blair's resolve to align Britain with the United States at dicey moments.

Other examples of Blair's willingness to take large risks included his strong advocacy of using force against Serbia during the conflict over Kosovo. He alone among NATO leaders was prepared to commit ground troops, and his tough line put Britain at the center of events there and influenced the outcome.

According to people who know him well and have his confidence, the Gladstonian side of Blair is mixed with a strong sense of realpolitik and a sharp calculation of the affect of whatever he may do on British power. "It's my job to protect and project British power," he told one such person.

To date, Blair's assumption that his special tie to the White House, whoever the occupant may be, sustains and enhances Britain's influence in Europe and the world has not been borne out. Granted, his role in maneuvering George Bush toward a multilateral approach to Iraq in the fall of 2002 was pivotal, more so possibly than even Colin Powell's. In the end, however, this expedient changed nothing. Bush had decided to make war with or without international support.

The risks that Blair had been running were self-evident. Problems and disagreements with Washington that lay just beneath the surface abruptly became controversial and politically awkward. The acute sources of discord involved the Middle East, Iran, missile defense, space, and the administration's disdain for arms-control agreements along with its perceived indifference to the nuclear threshold and other opinions.

The problem arising from Blair's robust backing of Bush's drive to oust Saddam Hussein extended well beyond his political base. A procession of British notables publicly deplored the idea of invading Iraq. They included two former chiefs of the defense staff and Sir Michael Quinlan, for many years the senior professional in the Ministry of Defense and a universally respected authority. Blair was stung by being persistently referred to in some newspapers as Bush's poodle.

From the start, Blair was supported by the heavily circulated newspapers of Rupert Murdoch and Conrad Black. Black is a convinced Tory, Murdoch a figure of the hard right. Blair would lose the support of both had he seemed even to be flirting with the idea of breaking with Bush over a security issue like Iraq.

After 9/11, a small group of officials, backed by the President, set about taking control of Washington's national security apparatus. Steps to marginalize the structure of diplomacy, laws, alliances, and multinational bodies had begun prior to 9/11, but then went forward all but unchecked as the President, lifted politically by the event, found his voice. The scope of the change wrought by Bush's inner circle—people called neo-cons by the press but seen elsewhere as elements of the hard right—defies immediate comprehension. All or most of what they've done is unlikely to last, but could take a long time to undo.

Who has benefited from the change and whose larger interests have been damaged remains unclear. A few things are certain. The damage to the European Union and its quest for greater cohesion won't be reparable for a very long time.

Differences between key EU capitals over the U.S. approach to Iraq created some splits that could be lasting and could widen. Parenthetically, the Bush administration is the first since post–World War II days that doesn't support a strong and cohesive grouping of European states. The EU's foreign assistance—more than half the world total—doesn't count for much in the Bush-Cheney view of what matters; neither does its position as America's most important economic partner.

Another loser was NATO, already weakened by the absence of a clear vocation and having become a work in progress. The conflict underlined the administration's lack of commitment to the alliance and its questionable relevance to the intersecting threats of terrorism and weapons of mass destruction. However, the war did leave behind a role for which NATO was ideally suited—providing the internal security that Iraq must have while the process of stabilizing the society and building institutions went forward. But the administration began life with strong reservations about NATO that haven't changed.

China is one of the very few winners; after initially being cast as designated adversary by the Cheney-Rumsfeld wing of the administration, it emerged post-9/11 as an ally in the campaign against terrorism, and quietly supported the war against Iraq. Shortly after the war was over, the White House said it would not offer a UN resolution condemning China for human rights abuses, the first time since the 1989 massacre in Tiananmen Square that the United States has not tried to censure Beijing. Long-term, China may see the United States as a threat to its coveted role as the dominant power in Northeast Asia.

The close bilateral ties with Berlin, Moscow, and Paris that remain central to American interests were hard hit by the war with Iraq. Although the Bush-Putin relationship wasn't as badly shaken as it might have been, Putin's considerable political skills will be sorely tested. The war weakened Moscow's pro-Western bloc, provoked a resurgence of anti-Americanism in the country, and further toughened Russia's hard-liners and nationalists. Putin joined the chorus at one point, blaming Washington for destabilizing the world order. But the White House cut him more slack than it did others who opposed the war. It may continue to do so, depending on whether Bush and Putin are able to separate their personal relationship from disagreements that can be expected to lie ahead. Bush tends to see the relationship in isolation from Russia itself. Indeed, he has no Russia policy. Saying all the right things to Bush at summit meetings counts for a lot. Bush is known to feel that Putin is someone he can talk to without connecting the dots. It's about him and Putin, much less so about the United States and Russia. Interestingly, when in the middle of a political campaign Gerhard Schroeder announced his opposition to war with Iraq, Bush called Putin to complain and discuss the matter.

Mending the often troubled, always edgy U.S.–French relationship may be, at best, a gradual process. Mixed American feelings about France—a difficult ally but in the end one of the family—has given way to a pervasive Francophobia. French bashing is very much the fashion, especially on the hard right. And in May 2003, the animosity between Paris and Washington was dramatized by a formal protest from the French government against what it called "an organized campaign of disinformation" about France that, it said, had been under way within the Bush administration over the previous nine months. The complaint referred to numerous newspaper articles, citing anonymous administration officials as sources. The pieces were all clearly aimed at angering readers, and in some cases shocking them, too. For example, on May 6, an article in the *Washington Times* cited "an American intelligence official" as saying that France had helped Iraqi leaders wanted by the United States to escape to Europe by providing them with French passports. When asked about the story by the press, the White House, State Department, and CIA said they had no such information.[6] In France, mixed feelings about America itself—admiration mixed with traditional derision—has given way to something much narrower: a universal but pronounced hostility toward Bush.

Repairing the differences with Germany won't take nearly as long. After having studiously ignored Berlin for a time, Washington accepted the obvious need to restore the link, although it is likely to be less sturdy and routinely serviceable than before. But the Germans, like the French and most other Europeans, share an aversion to what they see as an expanding religious zealotry in America. And they tend to see this religiosity as related to what they also see as a disturbing post-9/11 acceptance by Americans of infringements on their constitutional rights.

There is a related concern, publicly expressed in May 2003 by Rubens A. Barbosa, Brazil's ambassador to the United States, that Americans, increasingly aware of their country's imperial bearing, are "softening demands that its conduct abroad be fully consistent with the values proclaimed by U.S. society as a whole."[7] He could have added that America's main strength lies in what it stands for and is seen to stand for. The damage from the Iraq issue to America's standing in Europe was heavy and will begin to subside only if and when Washington softens its approach to the world by becoming less unilateral and threatening and more inclined to operate with sensitivity to the views of others.

Members of the so-called neo-con faction would disagree; they argue that exercising America's special responsibilities in a Hobbesian world dictates a hard-nosed policy like Bush's. They contrast hard power—America's surpassing military power and versatility—with soft power. By that, they mean Europe's preference for passive defenses based on agreements among nations; preventive diplomacy conducted under the auspices of multilateral institutions; military transparency and exchanges of surveillance data; and military forces capable of modest operations. For a half century, the United States, with a somewhat different set of special responsibilities, was the chief sponsor and architect of soft-power arrangements while also deploying formidable hard power. But Bush and his inner circle have treated soft power dismissively.

European countries regard the instruments of soft power as the first line of defense against terrorism. Raw military power, they think, is occasionally useful but always secondary. Britain, which fought terrorists in Northern Ireland for thirty or so years and in Malaya for a dozen, doesn't see that kind of struggle as a "war against terrorism," but rather as a campaign. Wars have structure and a timeline. They begin and they end. Terrorists, if neutralized, may go underground and reappear unexpectedly one day.

Terrorism is generally seen as part of a larger problem, not a single problem. Thus far, however, Washington's concern with the causes of terrorism has been minimal. The administration's focus on threats emanating from the three "axis of evil" states, plus a few others, has seemed disturbingly consistent with its apparent indifference to a tense and more volatile environment.

In less than two years, Bush's presidency has experienced the post–Cold War era's first two defining events: the attacks on 9/11 and the war in Iraq. "In the world we have entered," he said, "the only path to safety is the path of action. And this nation will act."[8] How Bush and Cheney decide to act henceforth is likely to shape the course of events to come.

Whether the United States will emerge from the experience in Iraq as a net winner or loser remains unclear. The administration gambled by sending a large force halfway around the world to wage war in a harsh environment against forces that might have used chemical or even biological weapons. The war was won swiftly and with fewer losses of American life than probably expected. Nothing succeeds like success, and the administration felt more than vindicated. Its supporters and much of the country took pride from what transpired in Iraq.

However, the administration was unprepared for the war, except militarily. The post-conflict phase of providing security, competent public services, and an indigenous political structure was largely unplanned and improvisational. The lack of preparation extended even to a failure to secure and protect Iraqi nuclear facilities. Seven of them were damaged or destroyed by looting. Technical documents, sensitive equipment, and barrels of uranium oxide were reported to have been stolen. Radioactive poisoning befell many of the looters. One site contained more than 500 tons of natural uranium and nearly 2 tons of low-enriched uranium, along with smaller amounts of highly radioactive cesium, cobalt, and strontium.

The war was never popular elsewhere, and neither the vanquishing of an obscenely evil regime nor the brevity of the campaign offset the argument that a casus belli had never been established; that Iraq's link to terrorism lay somewhere between minimal and nonexistent; that Washington had not allowed UN inspectors the time they should have had to determine whether Iraqi WMD amounted to a serious threat. It's unclear whether the war's impact will prove a net plus in reducing terrorism or provide a recruiting bonanza for violence and anti-Americanism in the Arab world and beyond. There is a better than even chance that the war will not inhibit the spread of unconventional weapons but rather encourage it.

In the Arab world and Europe, people watching television saw more of the impact of the war on Iraqi life than did American audiences, which were kept in closer touch with the battlefield. Scenes in Baghdad of hospitals trying to cope with the streams of wounded created an anger and frustration that dogged the military campaign and may haunt its aftermath.

The end of hostilities coincided with heavy verbal artillery fire from Washington directed toward Damascus. Some of the complaints about Syria's role were valid and, it seemed, taken aboard by the leadership in Damascus. Others were unpersuasive and accompanied by a veiled threat of retribution; that was an awkward overreaction, not to mention badly timed—and it, too, was resented in the Arab world. All of the above, some of it exaggerated in the retelling by America bashers, produced a harsh judgment of Washington.

Chapter 6

Opportunities Redux

Thus far, the post-9/11 experience, as Bush shaped it, has skewed America's perceptions of security, along with its place and role in the world. Allies are watching the United States through a lens as hostile as that of predictable America bashers. It didn't all start with Bush, though. Well before his arrival, there was comment, especially in Europe, that Washington had become increasingly tone deaf and was confusing consultation with edicts. European governments had grievances, some legitimate, others more imaginary than real. But the complaining was rarely shrill; most capitals were hardly surprised to see the one remaining superpower sometimes taking more for granted than it should.

What much or most of the world now thinks it sees in America is a post-Iraq aura of triumphalism, along with a heavy self-satisfaction that clouds the society's view of itself. Curiously, the post–World War II period had little self-congratulatory spirit. There was a pervasive sense of satisfaction mixed with relief that the United States and its allies had at last won the war, but Americans began to feel culturally insecure, possibly because the war had done a lot to end their isolation. Also, they had taken the lead in building multinational institutions like the UN and NATO, and as a society were looking more carefully at the world and at what was going on around them. They began learning more about other countries and wondering how America and Americans looked to these societies, especially Europe and most especially France, a supposed citadel of culture and elevated thought.

Books with titles like *As Others See Us* began to appear. The Cold War was under way, and Americans worried about the Communist bloc's intentions and the Soviet atom bomb. Several newspapers, not just a diminishing few, maintained correspondents in numerous foreign capitals. The coverage of foreign news was broader and closely read. Today, the interest in and hence the coverage of hard news has fallen off, and the line between entertainment and hard news has dimmed.

Fortuitously, the major opportunities that lay before Bush post-9/11 resurfaced as fighting in Iraq ended. The swift victory strengthened Bush's already tight hold on his power base, thereby allowing him to consider taking steps that might otherwise have collided with Karl Rove's reelection strategy. Restarting the Middle East peace process on terms other than Sharon's offered the most important and most immediate example. Building bridges to Iran's reformist government provided another, and one equally unpopular with Israel's Likud party and its American allies. But policy toward Iran continued to have few sensible attributes; it remained a muddle.

North Korea was a more immediate and worrisome problem. The administration clearly hoped that Iraq's experience would have a sobering effect on the leadership, and it probably did. Kim Jong Il must have concluded that with Bush, what you see is what you get. Kim had already experienced insults and the "axis of evil" anathema. And he had had time to consider the prevention/preemption doctrine and whether Bush actually did connect it to Iraqi WMD. If so, he had to assume that his country could be the next candidate for regime change. Many Korea watchers felt that even before the war in Iraq, Kim Jong Il had concluded that only by developing a nuclear deterrent could he hope to head off the worst. Skating quite so close to the brink would at an earlier stage have been counter-intuitive for either Kim or his father. Their principal goal was, and is, a security guarantee from the United States and, with it, the freedom to build the North Korean economy with the help of Japan, South Korea, and financial institutions. Their unconventional weapons programs were there mainly to be bargained away, ideally for the guarantee. But the Bush approach to the world and especially to North Korea affected the calculation. It raised the question of whether Kim Jong Il would equate his survival with a capacity to deter a military attack from America. In the bargain, creating a tool of that kind might be seen by Kim as a way of improving access to capital, energy, and prestige.

In the Middle East, America's policy struck allies as being a prisoner of domestic politics and acquiescing in the spread of Israeli settlements. Until late May 2003, all sides were doubtful that the White House would press for a resolution of the Palestine problem on terms significantly less one-sided than Sharon's. Bush's political calendar pointed the other way. His supposed support for the famous road map had been judged another brief tactical interlude, designed to give Tony Blair, among its foremost advocates, a fig leaf during the parliamentary debate on the war.

But some things had changed. During the run-up to the war in Iraq, Bush had promised a few of the regional leaders that he would make a serious effort to restart the peace process. And he had said as much to Blair. He also held some strong cards; none of his predecessors was as trusted by an Israeli government as he had become. Also, a laudable initiative in the Middle East could have been seen in the White House as a way to offset the administration's obvious and inexplicable failure to develop a coherent plan for the war's aftermath.

The harsh critique of this failure was accompanied by accusations that the Bush team had misrepresented intelligence about the supposed link between Iraq and al-Qaeda and about Saddam's supposed stock of unconventional weapons. Some officials from within the intelligence community took their complaints to the press. Cheney and his chief of staff, "Scooter" Libby, were singled out. During most of the year preceding the war, they reportedly made "multiple trips" to the CIA, where they questioned analysts about Iraq's unconventional weapons and alleged links to al-Qaeda. By one account, Cheney and Libby were "creating an environment in which some analysts felt . . . pressured to make their assessments fit with the Bush administsration's policy objectives."[1]

An official from the Defense Intelligence Agency who said he was privy to all the intelligence on Iraq was quoted as saying, "The American people were manipulated." Intelligence professionals were stirred up enough to form a group, Veteran Intelligence Professionals for Sanity. And they wrote to Bush to protest what they called "a policy and intelligence fiasco of monumental proportions."[2]

Bush then became part of the story. A statement that he made in the Rose Garden in September 2002 was noted by the *Washington Post* as conflicting with a cautionary intelligence report. "The Iraqi regime," Bush said, "possesses biological and chemical weapons, [and] is building the facilities necessary to make more biological and chemical weapons." But according to the *Washington Post*'s story, a Defense Intelligence Agency report on chemical weapons, widely distributed to administration policymakers at this time, stated that there was "no reliable information on whether Iraq is producing or stockpiling chemical weapons or whether Iraq has or will establish its chemical agent production facilities."[3]

Bush's statement was seen as part of the campaign to acquire Congressional support for authorizing military action against Iraq. But during the run-up to the war, the intelligence community had no direct evidence to support a conclusion about Iraq's unconventional weapons. There was little hard information, mainly because UN weapons inspectors had left Iraq in 1998.[4]

It was early in the war's shrill postmortems that Bush pronounced himself ready for evenhanded peacemaking in the Middle East, after twenty-eight months of observing the violence there from the sidelines. The postwar muddle in Iraq may have altered his political calculus. Discharging a debt to Tony Blair could have partially explained the move, although Whitehall was as surprised by Bush's radical change of course as most of Washington was. Whatever the reasons, Bush did commit himself and his office; he was taking on a heavy obligation, and with it a heavy risk. Only if he personally involved himself for as long as it took and deployed the full authority of his office would a balanced agreement at last become attainable.

Whether Bush would play a role so out of character and stay the course wasn't just the key variable but also the major uncertainty. A well-sourced article in the *Washington Post* quoted one administration official as saying, "He does not have the knowledge or the patience to learn this issue enough to have an end destination in mind." This official, along with others, was reported as being concerned that Bush would expect the other parties in the region to figure out "the hard questions without firm intervention by the United States [and] ultimately leave the peace process adrift."[5] Flynt L. Leverett, who until March 2003 was the senior director for Israeli-Palestinian affairs on the National Security Council, said, "They [White House officials] went into this thinking they were serious. But they had no idea what being serious would mean."[6]

As for Palestine's new prime minister, Mahmoud Abbas, better known as Abu Mazen, the scale of his task can't be overstated. Although tough and well intentioned, Abbas is the weakest of the various players. He must find a way of imposing his authority on the terrorist groups, not just for a circumscribed period of time but permanently. Accomplishing that, however, and gaining the confidence of his deeply suspicious, deeply cynical people will depend on whether he shows that he can improve their lives and end the Israeli occupation. A great many Palestinians have more confidence in Arafat, who will use his considerable resourcefulness to recapture the role of spoiler.

All of this raises the question of what Israel's leadership is prepared to give up in return for movement toward stability and a settlement. Sharon can talk about ending the occupation, but what would that mean? Removing the illegal settlements? Some or most of the other settlements? Will Israel's security continue to be seen as requiring separation between Palestinian towns and cities?

Finally, it was never easy to imagine much in the way of progress emerging from the sequential, reciprocal steps envisaged by the road map. Palestine has been chopped into pieces, few of which are controlled by Palestinians. A patchwork of these isolated enclaves cobbled into a so-called state would be separated by Israeli settlements and/or military checkpoints, and bear little resemblance to a Palestinian state.

A resolution of this tortured problem, when and if there is one, will require a comprehensive agreement that guarantees Israel's security and establishes a viable Palestinian state. In 2002, Saudi Arabia's Crown Prince Abdullah proposed a long step in that direction. It was known as full return for full peace, meaning that Israel would withdraw to the borders that existed prior to the Six-Day War in 1967 and the Arab countries would grant formal recognition to Israel.

By not pushing Bush as hard as they might have on the Middle East, Blair and Powell may still be seen historically as political casualties of his policies there. We cannot be entirely sure about what motivated Blair on Iraq. We know that he fully accepted the proposition that Britain can punch above its weight only if closely linked, if not joined at the hip, to the United States. But despite Blair's steadfast support for Bush, Britain had not been punching above its weight.

Powell, like Blair, is likely to be seen as having been exploited. The State Department, which always had custodial responsibility for policy in the Near East, lost it to a cabal of resourceful ideologues across the Potomac River. But Powell, fully aware of this group's intentions, should have threatened resignation before yielding control. If State could surrender oversight of the Middle East, why would it not have to yield management of other sectors of foreign policy?

American military power is constantly growing although the country's overall security may be declining, if only because its priorities are skewed and unbalanced. For example, the United States invests ever more heavily in a defense establishment whose redundancy exceeds realistic threat assessments, but disdains other essential attributes of power. Washington is steadfastly reluctant to pursue alternate sources of energy, even though the country is highly vulnerable to fluctuations in the price of oil. Another example is nuclear weapons. In opposing the spread of these and other weapons of mass destruction, Washington takes issue strongly with the programs of other countries, but not Israel's. The deployment by Israel of nuclear weapons is beyond reproach in Washington, even though it gives other countries in the region an incentive to develop their own WMD programs; if they feel a need to legitimize such programs, they cite American hypocrisy.

In justifying the decision to make war on Iraq, George Bush would remind us that he had taken an oath to defend the security of the United States and that Saddam Hussein posed an imminent threat to the country. He didn't. Various other threats were—are—imminent, some more so than others, some more lethal than others. An attack, say, with biological and/or chemical weapons might take as many lives as were lost on September 11, but would probably fall well short of that number. The destructive effect of even a primitive, low-yield nuclear weapon, however, would vastly exceed any of the other horrors that might menace America. And the most serious single threat lies in the numerous nuclear weapons and the quantities of fissile material that are not fully secure or beyond the reach of terrorists.

Most of these "loose nukes" and the fissile material of concern are Russian, widely scattered in storage sites; the security of a great many of the sites is far from adequate, let alone reliable. Discouraging thefts or illicit sales of the weapons and material is a tough, exacting problem. The efforts to cope with it—so-called cooperative threat reduction (CTR) programs— are proving arduous, expensive, and necessarily long-term. They are also politically demanding and even intrusive, since they center on helping, and to a degree persuading, Russia to improve the safety and security of its nuclear weapons.

The U.S. government has been running CTR programs for more than a decade. The most conspicuous of them was sponsored by Senator Richard Lugar and former Senator Sam Nunn in the early 1990s. To date, thousands of nuclear weapons and hundreds of missile systems, along with strategic aircraft, have been destroyed. A good deal of nuclear weapons-grade material and a number of the devices themselves have been made more secure.

A lot has been accomplished, but not nearly enough. Roughly half of Russia's weapons-grade material is judged insufficiently secure, hence insecure. By the end of fiscal year 2002, only 37 percent of the potentially vulnerable nuclear material in Russia was protected by security upgrades. Less than one sixth of Russia's stockpile of highly enriched uranium had been destroyed. [7]

"The most effective, least expensive way to prevent nuclear terrorism is to secure nuclear weapons and materials at the source," said Senator Nunn. "Acquiring weapons and materials is the hardest step for the terrorists to take and easiest step for us to stop."[8]

It can be persuasively argued that the investment in CTR programs is at least as good a return on the defense-related dollar as any. However, the funding for them has been uneven and far from adequate. For fiscal year 2004, the President's request amounted to just one quarter of 1 percent of total U.S. defense spending. In 2001, a bipartisan task force led by former senator Howard Baker and former White House counsel Lloyd Cutler stated that "the most urgent unmet national security threat to the United States . . . is the danger that weapons of mass-destruction or weapons-usable material in Russia could be stolen and sold to terrorists or hostile nation states." The report warned of delays in payments to guards at nuclear facilities; breakdowns in command structures, including units that control weapons or guard weapons-usable material; and inadequate budgets for protection of stockpiles and laboratories.[9] It cited "impressive results so far" in current nonproliferation programs but concluded that if funding were not increased, there would be an "unacceptable risk of failure" that could lead to "catastrophic consequences."[10]

Although the Bush administration, in concert with other members of the G-8 group of nations, agreed to invest more money, it hasn't given Nunn-Lugar and the other CTR programs much high-level attention. There is no mechanism within the government for targeting the available funds coherently or coordinating the several cabinet departments involved in CTR. These relevant agencies are, in the bureaucratic jargon, "stovepiped"—meaning they internalize what they do, and don't interact, at least not usefully, with others performing similar work.

Congressional politics complicate the overall effort. CTR is seen in the House of Representatives as "a Senate program," especially given the Nunn-Lugar association. Many Republican members of the House regard the programs skeptically and even derisively. They charge that large sums of money are thrown at CTR, then lost track of and wasted. However, they do not object to the vastly greater sums made available to missile defense, money that much of the national security community regards as extravagant and misspent. Russia's assistance to Iran's nuclear program is used by House Republicans to justify their reservations about CTR programs. They have blocked supplemental appropriations for CTR several times.

Spotty Russian cooperation with CTR is another problem. Moscow's official line is that Russian standards of nuclear safety and security are at least as high as those of the United States and Europe, but that lack of domestic funding has prevented fully implementing them. There is unavoidable tension between the need to maintain the dignity of the Russian state and having to put Minatom and the security services under pressure to play a serious role in cooperative efforts to manage the loose-nukes problem.

There have been many documented cases of theft of kilogram quantities of weapons-usable material. The IAEA has a database that cites eighteen incidents involving seizure of stolen HEU or plutonium.[11] Putin knows what should be done, but he is somewhat constrained by the bureaucratic drag in Moscow. The Foreign Ministry is weak, Minatom very strong, and the security services, not surprisingly, tend to equate protecting their turf with protecting the secrecy of Russia's weapons and how they are deployed.

This is a fundamental problem, broader than CTR but also affecting everyone's security. Quite simply, CTR and other efforts aimed at controlling the number and distribution of nuclear weapons need a political structure. Or call it process. Without this, the programs don't have legs. The arms-control process provided structure. Agreements had to be verified with intrusive measures. There was an array of agreed understandings. The process has now all but lapsed and, with it, the structure. Among the casualties is transparency, the absence of which breeds excessive caution—worst-case analysis which in turn leads to grossly incorrect estimates of the other party's military assets. Not unreasonably, Russians ask themselves why they, the weaker party, should give even well-intentioned Americans access to sensitive facilities if there is no reciprocity. To take one of many examples, Russia doesn't know how much HEU the United States has in storage, because that information is still seen as sensitive and not to be shared. Nor has Washington ever come clean on its biological weapons program. In short, even in the case of so worthy a project as CTR, there must be something in it for the other party. Russia's leadership doesn't like agreements that do not impose precise obligations on the parties, all parties.

In May 2002, Bush and Putin signed a treaty in Moscow— the Strategic Offensive Reductions Treaty—that was advertised as having set a limit on deployed warheads. But the agreement provided neither actual limits nor a whiff of process. It was toothless, although all parties appeared to get something. Putin and Colin Powell had pressed for a written agreement, and after a good deal of wrangling in Washington they got one. But the Bush team was determined that whatever was agreed to would not inhibit any part of the Pentagon's strategic planning. Hence, the text was meager and indulgent. Not a single missile launcher or warhead would have to be destroyed under the agreement. Each side was allowed to carry out reductions in warheads at its own pace, or even halt reductions and rebuild its force. Washington insisted on having, as it's called, a reconstitution capability as a hedge against threats that might one day be posed by China or a retrograde Russia.[12]

An escape clause allowed withdrawal on just three months notice. The only constraint was that each side could have no more than 1,700 to 2,200 weapons deployed at the end of 2012, when the treaty expired. And those were the numbers called for by the Pentagon in its Nuclear Posture Review of 2002. Moreover, at the end of 2012, each party would be free to deploy as many weapons as it chose unless the agreement was extended.

As for tightening control of loose nukes, the agreement contributed nothing. Indeed critics could argue that it might have further complicated the problem, since the deactivated warheads, instead of being disabled, would be moved into storage facilities and possibly remain as targets for terrorists. That danger is probably more apparent than real since terrorists are presumably less intent on trying to steal a large strategic weapon than a much smaller tactical one, of which there are many more in Russia. We don't know how many. Estimates have varied between 4,000 and 15,000, and besides being more portable, these weapons are thought to be less protected by computerized anti-use codes.

What seems clear is that if the Moscow agreement had provided for destruction of strategic warheads, a useful precedent would have been set. The logical follow-up step could have been a negotiation aimed at getting rid of all or most of the tactical weapons in storage.[13]

There will never be a better time for getting these nuclear weapons that matter most—Russia's—under control. No longer does a superpower rivalry dictate parity at high-force levels and an unending cycle of force improvement. Also, America has all the advantages in strategic weapons, and Russia cannot afford to sustain what it has. Its increasingly obsolescent, worn-down missile forces are shrinking to low levels.

Ironically, the president who did most to control nuclear weapons was George Bush senior. He and his team negotiated the Strategic Arms Reduction Treaties (START) I and II. They also withdrew most of the tactical nuclear weapons deployed abroad, leaving behind just a symbolic few. A presidential directive in September 1991 ordered the armed forces to eliminate the entire inventory of ground-launched theater nuclear weapons; and tactical nuclear weapons from all surface ships, attack submarines, and land-based naval aircraft bases. America's strategic bombers would stand down from their "alert postures" and their nuclear weapons would be removed and stored in secure areas. Other steps included halting the nuclear short-range-attack missile program. And then, strongly encouraged by a Democratic Congress, this administration also announced a moratorium on testing of nuclear weapons. It also began the funding for the Nunn-Lugar program.

Another irony borne out by experience is that serious progress in arms control is best accomplished when Washington's power structure mixes a moderate Republican president with a Democratic Congress. Nothing else really works. Democrats tend to support arms control, but a Democrat in the White House usually has great difficulty in maneuvering an arms-control proposal past Congress. Right-wing Republicans can be relied on to attack it as unverifiable or favoring the other party to the negotiation or otherwise damaging national security. A moderate Republican president can try moving the arms-control process along at little risk that Democrats in Congress will oppose him. And right-wing Republicans, however hostile to arms-control agreements, are reluctant to undermine a president who is nominally one of their tribe.

Moderates feel that among the lessons of the Cold War was that nuclear weapons do not constitute usable military power. Their role then was to deter an attack, however improbable, from other such weapons. That is still true, at least as seen by the larger part of the national security community and most foreign governments. Within the dominant wing of the Republican party, however, moderation is not the fashion and hasn't been for quite some time. Rumsfeld, Wolfowitz, and some of their colleagues take a broader, more relaxed view of nuclear weapons. And they intend, according to published reports, to produce and deploy a thermonuclear "bunker-buster," a bomb that would destroy hardened, deeply buried targets. The weapon would be thousands of times more powerful than the conventional bunker-busters that were used to bomb sites in Iraq where Saddam Hussein might have been.[14]

Within and beyond Congress, opponents of the Robust Nuclear Earth Penetrator, as the bunker-buster device is called, argue that it would throw up enormous clouds of deadly radioactive dust, not to mention causing widespread destruction. Many weapons specialists argue that buried bunkers can be destroyed with conventional munitions or by using troops to attack entrances, air shafts, and communications cables.

As on many other issues that have been pushed by this Pentagon's civilian leadership, the uniformed military takes a contrary view. "If you can find somebody in a uniform in the Defense Department who can talk about a new need [for nuclear bunker-busters] without laughing, I'll buy him a cup of coffee," said Robert Peurifoy, a retired vice president of Sandia National Laboratory in New Mexico, a lab that would play a role in the project.

"I've talked to the military extensively, and I don't know anybody in the military who thinks they need a nuclear weapon to accomplish this," said Democratic Congresswoman Ellen Tauscher, whose district includes the Lawrence Livermore National Laboratory. She and Representative John Spratt, a Democrat and fellow member of the Armed Services Committee, are leading the opposition to the weapon in the House.[15]

Among the strongest advocates is Representative Duncan

Hunter, a Republican from San Diego and chairman of that committee. "You have to have the ability to go after the leaders of a military activity against the United States," he has said. "Having . . . bunker-buster capability is an important aspect of deterrence."[16]

Among the pivotal questions is whether this novel weapon would have to be tested prior to being deployed. Its partisans say no, on the grounds that it would be a modification of a smaller existing bomb. Skeptics and outright opponents, some of them weapons specialists, see an obvious need to test in order to measure blast, radiation, and other effects. Any weapon, they argue, that is supposed to perform the mission established for this one would have to be tested.

A resumption of nuclear testing by the United States would be both a peremptory and provocative act, because it would be perceived universally as lowering the nuclear threshold and putting great pressure on the Non-Proliferation Treaty. Put differently, cancellation of the Anti-Ballistic Treaty and early steps toward a national missile defense could be seen by Putin and others in Moscow as manageable over time, especially if the missile defense program eventually falls of its own weight, as Putin may think it will. But a resumption of testing would be judged an unambiguously destabilizing event, as would the creation of a new family of nuclear weapons.

The largest of the ironies in the generally small-minded treatment of nuclear weapons over the past quarter century is that they probably threaten the United States more than any other party. The quality, destructive power, and versatility of American nuclear forces greatly exceed anyone else's. And the United States deploys the strongest conventional forces the world has seen. If only for this reason, Washington should be the foremost advocate of a strict nonproliferation regime; only proliferation could threaten to narrow America's overwhelming advantage. The greater reason to treat nonproliferation as a foremost national priority lies in the obvious and fearsome possibilities inherent in the spread of nuclear weapons. Developing and testing another one would amount to folly, another self-injurious act and a disservice to the rest of the world.

Bush and the kindred spirits who advise him are not impressed by history. They seem to feel that America's world position—that mix of unexampled political, economic, and military power—is more than a match for centuries of history. But their confident assumptions are not likely to be borne out even partially unless they take the politically brave, counterintuitive decisions of the kind that complicate life for leadership. Using maximum pressure to influence and resolve the Palestine situation would promote security in the region for all sides, including Israel, and would send a message that the United States is serious about solving serious problems—problems that threaten parties in and out of the region and provide fuel for terrorists.

Granted, the Middle East is difficult and complex. So are the dilemmas presented by Iran and North Korea. Iran, not Iraq, is the key to stability in the region they share. Iraq will always be threatened, or feel threatened, by an unstable but stronger Iran. Yet Iran is pulled more strongly by pro-Western sentiment and reformist political pressures than any state in that part of the world. Washington can and should be playing a long game there.

It wasn't lost on North Korea's oppressive regime that the Iraqi campaign involved less than a sixth of America's total armed forces. Thus, prospects for talks between Pyongyang and Washington a bit closer to Bush's terms stood a better chance of going forward, provided Washington could avoid allowing hubris to forestall a deal that met the interests that each side considered vital.

The problem posed by Pakistan remains objectively more difficult than any of these others, much harder to think through. The Bush people who matter most seem not to have preoccupied themselves with the danger that another war between India and Pakistan could break out and, besides eclipsing other problems, including Iraq, might even involve nuclear weapons. At moments, they did focus hard when the situation in the subcontinent seemed on the verge of erupting; otherwise, the far less urgent, far less threatening problem of Iraq crowded out other issues and other interests.

America's oldest allies continue to wonder why the administration has laid siege to the world order. International law and the web of multinational institutions are inherently useful to the United States because of its special responsibilities to discourage conflict and instability. The Bush preference for operating unilaterally, or at times through ad hoc "coalitions of the willing," ignores a basic fact of international life: America and the rest of the world are interdependent, and have been, to one degree or another, for a long time. To take one in an extensive list of examples, the United States is the world's biggest debtor, its current account running nearly half again higher than its defense spending. Sustaining this state of affairs is likely to require not just fiscal discipline but multilateral cooperation. Meanwhile, the expanding and wholly unprecedented gulf between the United States and much of the rest of the world will reinforce the perverse effects on American life of Bush's radical economic and social policies.

The administration is trying to create reality, not deal with it. Continuing to do so may lead to the formation of a group, or coalition, of countries that openly distances itself from U.S. policies and actions. Put differently, when and if the administration begins to understand that its approach to the world isn't working, other countries may no longer be prepared to share with America the risks that ought to be taken and the problems that should be dealt with. If it does stay on course, the administration will make the world less stable and the United States a more insular and more vulnerable place.

Notes

All unattributed quotations come from personal
conversations with the author.

Chapter I. Opportunities Lost

1. Michael Donovan, "Engagement Before Invasion," Center for Defense Information, *CDI Weekly Defense Monitor* 7, no. 9, March 6, 2003.

2. Richard Cohen, "Amateur Hour at the White House," *Washington Post*, January 16, 2003, p. A19.

3. Jackson Diehl, "Accidental Imperialist," *International Herald Tribune*, December 31, 2002, p. 4.

4. U.S. Department of State, "Principal Themes on Missile Defense," memorandum, July 2002, http://www.ceip.org/files/projects/npp/resources/EmbassyCableNMD_copy.htm.

5. Michael Hirsh, "Bush and the World," *Foreign Affairs*, September–October 2002, p. 18.

6. General Wesley Clark, "An Army of One?" *Washington Monthly*, September 2002, http://www.washingtonmonthly.com/features/2001/0209/clark.html.

7. Karen DeYoung and Mike Allen, "Bush Shifts Strategy from Deterrence to Dominance," *Washington Post*, September 21, 2002, p. A01.

8. Anatol Lieven, "The Push for War," *London Review of Books*, October 3, 2002, p. 3.

9. Michael Dobbs, "N. Korea Tests Policy of Preemption," *Washington Post*, January 6, 2003, p. 1.

10. White House, Office of the Press Secretary, June 1, 2002.

11. Statement by Donald Rumsfeld released by the Department of Defense, September 9, 2002.

12. Ivan Safranchuk, "The U.S. National Security Strategy: A Russian Perception," *CDI Russia Weekly*, no. 224, September 27, 2002.

13. Frank Rich, "Group Therapy at Ground Therapy," *New York Times*, January 4, 2003, p. 27.

14. David Rogers, "Assertive President Engineers a Shift in Capital's Power," *Wall Street Journal*, October 22, 2002, pp. 1, 4.

15. Ibid.

16. Dana Milbank and Dan Morgan, "Bush, Hill Leaders Clash on Spending: President Would Veto New Emergency Funds," *Washington Post*, November 7, 2001, p. 1.

17. Laura Blumenfeld, "Former Aide Takes Aim at War on Terror," *Washington Post*, June 16, 2003, p. A1.

18. Rogers, "Assertive President Engineers a Shift."

19. Ibid.

20. Bob Woodward, "A Struggle for the President's Heart and Mind," *Washington Post*, November 17, 2002, p. 23.

21. "D-Day for Colin Powell," editorial, *New York Times*, July 28, 2002, http://www.nytimes.com/2002/07/28/opinion/28SUN1.html?ex=10561 68000&en=82106b24487610cb&ci=5070.

22. "How Will Israel Survive," msnbc.com/news, April 1, 2002, p. 10.

23. David E. Sanger, "Bush Says U.S. Is to Assume Stronger Role in Ending Violence," *New York Times*, April 5, 2002, p. 1.

24. Ibid., p. 34.

25. Alan Sipress, "Powell's Trip Leaves Mostly Doubts," *Washington Post*, April 17, 2002, p. A01.

26. David E. Sanger, "President Praises Effort by Powell in the Middle East," *New York Times*, April 19, 2002, p. 1.

27. David Wastel, *Sunday Telegraph*, July 7, 2002, p. 27.

28. Colin Powell with Joseph F. Persico, *My American Journey* (New York: Random House, 1995), p. 540.

29. "Rolling the President," editorial, *Washington Post*, September 25, 2002, p. A26.

30. Robert G. Kaiser, "Bush and Sharon Nearly Identical on Mideast Policy," *Washington Post*, February 9, 2003, p. 1.

31. Aluf Benn, "Sharon Says U.S. Should Also Disarm Iran, Libya and Syria," *Haaretz*, February 20, 2003, p. 1.

32. Edward Alden and Carola Hoyos, "A Loose Cannon," *Financial Times*, August 10–11, 2002, p. 7.

33. Ibid.

34. John Newhouse, *War and Peace in the Nuclear Age* (New York: Knopf, 1989), p. 259.

35. Ibid., p. 262.

Chapter 2. Iraq: A Dubious War

1. Elisabeth Bumiller, "March 2–8: International; War Press Conference," *New York Times*, March 9, 2003, p. 2.

2. Prepared testimony by Robert S. Mueller III before the Senate Select Committee on Intelligence, February 11, 2003.

3. "The Desert War—A Kind of Victory," BBC Radio, February 16, 1992.

4. Todd S. Purdum and Patrick E. Tyler, "Top Republicans Break with Bush on Iraq Strategy," *New York Times*, August 16, 2002, p. 1.

5. Elisabeth Bumiller and James Dao, "Cheney Says Peril of a Nuclear Iraq Justifies an Attack," *New York Times*, August 27, 2002, p. 1.

6. Glenn Kessler, "Powell Treads Carefully on Iraq Strategy," *Washington Post*, September 2, 2002, p. 1.

7. Brent Scowcroft, "Don't Attack Saddam," *Wall Street Journal*, August 15, 2002, p. A12.

8. Maureen Dowd, "Culture War with B-2's," *New York Times*, September 22, 2002, sec. 4, p. 12.

9. Ibid., sec. 4, p. 13.

10. Dana Milbank, "Powell Aide Disputes Views on Iraq," *Washington Post*, August 28, 2002, p. A16, citing a speech to the Economic Club of Florida, as reported in the *Tampa Tribune*.

11. Henry A. Kissinger, "Our Intervention in Iraq: How a Preemptive War Could Lead to a New International Order," *Washington Post*, August 12, 2002, p. A15.

12. Purdum and Tyler, "Top Republicans Break with Bush," p. 2.

13. Albert R. Hunt, "The Toughest Test: Après Saddam," *Wall Street Journal*, February 13, 2003, p. A13.

14. Michael Donovan, "Democracy in Iran?" Center for Defense Information, *CDI Weekly Defense Monitor* 6, no. 38, November 7, 2002.

15. Bob Woodward, "A Struggle for the President's Heart and Mind," *Washington Post*, November 17, 2002, p. 32.

16. Philip Stephens, "A Final Chance for Saddam to Evade America's Hawks," *Financial Times*, November 8, 2002, p. 19.

17. Elaine Sciolino, "The World; France and America, Perfect Together," *New York Times*, November 10, 2002, sec. 4, p. 14.

18. Kenneth Lieberthal, "Has China Become an Ally?" *New York Times*, October, 25, 2002, p. A35.

19. Dan Balz, "Gore Gives Warning on Iraq," *Washington Post*, September 24, 2002, p. 1.

20. Ibid.

21. "Imus Grills Lieberman, Redux," editorial, *Washington Times*, April 26, 2002, p. A22.

22. "Economically, It's Looking Grim," *The Economist*, November 9, 2002, p. 31.

23. E. J. Dionne Jr., "Democratic Catastrophe," *Washington Post*, November 7, 2002, p. A25.

24. Michael R. Gordon, "American Aides Split on Assessment of Iraq's Plans," *New York Times*, October 10, 2002, p. 1.

25. Ibid.
26. Warren B. Rudman and Gary Hart, "We Are Still Unprepared," *Washington Post*, November 5, 2002, p. 25.
27. Karen DeYoung, "Bush, Blair Decry Hussein; Iraqi Threat Is Real, They Say," *Washington Post*, September 8, 2002, p. A1.
28. Agence France-Presse wire story, "Saddam, 13 Others on 'Blacklist' for Postwar Trial," *Washington Times*, January 9, 2003, p. 11.
29. Philip Gordon and Michael O'Hanlon, "Dealing with Iraq," *Financial Times*, November 30, 2001, p. 15.
30. Roula Khalaf, "Saudis Pull Billions out of the U.S.," *Financial Times*, August 21, 2002, p. 1.
31. *Iraq: What Next?*, report of the Carnegie Endowment for International Peace, Joseph Cirincione, Jessica Tuchman Mathews, and George Perkovich, authors, January 2003, pp. 9–12.
32. Ibid.
33. John J. Mearshimer and Stephen M. Walt, "Keeping Saddam Hussein in a Box," *New York Times*, February 2, 2003, sec. 4, p. 15.
34. Michael R. Gordon and James Risen, "Report's Findings Undercut U.S. Argument," *New York Times*, January 28, 2003, p. 7.
35. Karen DeYoung, "A Skeptical U.N.," *Washington Post*, January 19, 2003, pp. 1, 20.
36. Julia Preston, "France Warns U.S. It Will Not Back Early War on Iraq," *New York Times*, January 21, 2003, p. 1.
37. "The Powell Doctrine Revisited," *The Economist*, February 1, 2002, p. 31.
38. Philip Stephens, "The Intelligence Furor Will Prove a Footnote in History," *Financial Times*, June 6, 2003, p. 13.
39. Thomas E. Ricks, "NATO Allies Trade Barbs over Iraq," *Washington Post*, February 9, 2003, pp. 1, 25.
40. Zbigniew Brzezinski, *CNN Late Edition*, March 9, 2003.
41. Laura d'Andrea Tyson, "A War That Lacks a Financial Strategy," *Financial Times*, February 25, 2003, p. 15.
42. George W. Bush, State of the Union Address, transcript at http://www.whitehouse.gov/news/releases/2003/01/20030128-19.html.
43. John Hendren, "A Huge Postwar Force Seen," *Los Angeles Times*, February 26, 2003, p. 1.
44. "Iraq and the Economy," editorial, *Washington Post*, September 20, 2002, p. A28.
45. Richard A. Oppel Jr., Diana B. Henriques, and Elizabeth Becker, "Who Will Put Iraq Back Together?" *New York Times*, March 23, 2003, sec. 3, pp. 1, 11.
46. *Guiding Principles for U.S. Post-Conflict Policy in Iraq*, report of an Independent Working Group Co-sponsored by the Council on Foreign

Relations and the James A. Baker III Institute for Public Policy of Rice University, Edward P. Djerjian and Frank G. Wisner, Co-Chairs, Rachel Bronson and Andrew S. Weiss, Project Co-Directors, February 2003, pp. 10–11.

47. George W. Bush, speech to American Enterprise Institute, February 26, 2003, transcript at http://www.whitehouse.gov/news/releases/2003/02/20030226-11.html.

48. Greg Miller, "Showdown with Iraq: Democracy Domino Theory 'Not Credible,' " *Los Angeles Times*, March 14, 2003, p. A1.

49. Robert D. Novak, "Calming Influences," *Washington Post*, August 12, 2002, p. 15.

Chapter 3. Iran in a Bad Neighborhood

1. Hugh Pope and Peter Waldman, "Iran's U.S.-Admiring Citizens Challenge Intentions of Hardline Islamic Leaders," *Wall Street Journal*, November 5, 2001, p. 1.

2. Michael Donovan, "A New Approach to Iran," Center for Defense Information, *CDI Terrorism Project*, May 23, 2002, www.cdi.org/terrorism/iran.cfm.

3. Vincent Cannistraro, analysis written for Intellibridge.

4. Glenn Kessler, "U.S. Changes Policy on Iranian Reform," *Washington Post*, July 23, 2002, p. 1.

5. Christopher de Bellaque, "Iran Changes Tack as Leader Likens Bush to Hitler," *Financial Times*, August 15, 2002, p. 2.

6. Guy Dinsmore and Najmeh Bozorgmehr, "Rumsfeld Pushes for Iran Action," *Financial Times*, May 30, 2003, p. 1.

7. Iran Radio, as reported by BBC, February 26, 2000, cited by Shahram Chubin in *Whither Iran? Reform, Domestic Politics and National Security*, Adelphi Paper 342, London, International Institute for Strategic Studies, April 2002, p. 25.

8. Ayatollah Khamenei, Voice of Iran, as reported by BBC, April 21, 1998, cited by Chubin in *Whither Iran?*

9. Elizabeth Rubin, "The Millimeter Revolution," *New York Times Magazine*, April 6, 2003, pp. 38–44.

10. Ibid., p. 41.

11. Babak Dehghanpisheh, "Khomeni's Children," *Newsweek International*, December 15, 2002.

12. Guy Dinsmore, "Iranian President Moves to Boost Powers with New Laws," *Financial Times*, August 29, 2002, p. 1.

13. Nagmeh Bozorgmehr, "Khatami Vents Anger on Clerics Backing Reform," *Financial Times*, May 22, 2003, p. 7.

14. Mahan Abedin, "The Origins of Iran's Reformist Elite," *Middle*

East Intelligence Bulletin, April 2003, at http://www.meib.org/articles/0304_iran. htm.

15. Chubin, *Whither Iran?*, p. 19.

16. John Newhouse and Thomas R. Pickering, "Getting Iran Right," *Washington Post*, December 28, 2001, p. A23.

17. Ibid.

18. George Perkovich, "Pressure Alone Will Not Deter Iran from Its Nuclear Path," *YaleGlobal Online*, June 10, 2003, at http://yaleglobal.yale.edu/display.article?id=1804.

19. Newhouse and Pickering, "Getting Iran Right," p. A23.

20. Ray Takeyh, "Re-imagining US-Iranian Relations," International Institute for Strategic Studies, *Survival* 3 (Autumn 2002): 28.

21. Ibid., p. 33.

22. Chubin, *Whither Iran?*, p. 62.

23. Anatol Lieven, "The Pressures on Pakistan," *Foreign Affairs*, January–February 2002, p. 110.

24. Farideh Farhi, "To Have or Not to Have? Iran's Domestic Debate on Nuclear Options," in *Iran's Nuclear Weapons Options: Issues and Analyses*, Washington, D.C., Nixon Center, January 2001, p. 39.

25. David E. Sanger, "In North Korea and Pakistan, Deep Roots of Nuclear Barter," *New York Times*, November 24, 2002, p. 1.

26. Interview with Mike Shuster, National Public Radio, November 7, 2001.

27. Steven Mufson, "The U.S. Worries About Pakistan's Nuclear Arms," *Washington Post*, November 4, 2001, p. A27.

28. Elisabeth Bumilller and Patrick E. Tyler, "Putin Questions U.S. Terror Allies," *New York Times*, November 23, 2002, pp. 1, 10.

29. Ibid.

30. Chubin, *Whither Iran?*, p. 72.

31. Ibid., p. 53.

32. Geoffrey Kemp, "Iran's Nuclear Options," in *Iran's Nuclear Weapons Options*, pp. 2, 15.

33. Michael R. Gordon, "Threats and Responses: Nuclear Programs; Inspectors View Nuclear Work at Iranian Site," *Washington Post*, February 23, 2003, p. 1.

34. Robert J. Einhorn and Gary Samore, "Ending Russia's Assistance to Iran's Nuclear Bomb," International Institute for Strategic Studies, *Survival* 44, no. 2 (Summer 2002): 52.

35. Ibid., p. 53.

36. Celeste A. Wallander, "Russia's Interest in Trading with the Axis of Evil," policy memo no. 248, Program on New Approaches to Russian Security, Center for Strategic and International Studies, October 2002, p. 6.

37. Stephen Sestanovich, "Dual Frustration: America, Russia and the Persian Gulf," *National Interest*, Winter 2002/03, p. 9.

38. Guy Dinmore, "Russia Ready to Supply N-Fuel to Iran," *Financial Times*, December 24, 2002, p. 5.

39. Wallander, "Russia's Interest in Trading," p. 8.

Chapter 4. Red Lines

1. Condoleezza Rice, "Promoting the National Interest," *Foreign Affairs* 79, no. 1(January/February 2000): 56.

2. Don Oberdorfer, *The Two Koreas* (New York: Basic Books, 2001), p. 253.

3. Scott Snyder, "Ending North Korea's Guerilla Tactics," *Financial Times*, February 3, 2003, p. 13.

4. Nancy E. Soderberg, "Escaping North Korea's Nuclear Trap," *New York Times*, February 12, 2003, p. 37.

5. Oberdorfer, *The Two Koreas*, pp. 277–78.

6. Ibid., p. 278.

7. Ibid., p. 280.

8. Ibid., p. 306.

9. Ibid.

10. Ibid., p. 320.

11. Ibid., p. 317.

12. Ibid., p. 57.

13. Leon Sigal, "North Korea Is No Iraq: Pyongyang's Negotiating Strategy," *Arms Control Today* 32, no. 10 (December 2002): 8.

14. Leon Sigal, "Negotiating an End to North Korea's Missile-Making," paper presented at LNCV–Korean Peninsula: Enhancing Stability and International Dialogue conference, Rome, June 1–2, 2000, p. 7.

15. Oberdorfer, *The Two Koreas*, p. 411.

16. Ibid., p. 419.

17. Ibid., pp. 422–23.

18. Ibid., p. 431.

19. Ibid., pp. 346–48.

20. Sigal, "North Korea Is No Iraq," p. 9.

21. Oberdorfer, *The Two Koreas*, p. 432.

22. Sigal, "North Korea Is No Iraq," p. 9.

23. Ibid.

24. Oberdorfer, *The Two Koreas*, pp. 436–37.

25. Ibid., p. 438.

26. Michael R. Gordon, "How Politics Sank Accord with North Korea," *New York Times*, March 6, 2001, p. 6.

27. Sigal, "North Korea Is No Iraq," p. 9.

28. Oberdorfer, *The Two Koreas*, p. 438.

29. Sigal, "North Korea Is No Iraq," p. 9.

30. Jake Tapper, "Did Bush Bungle Relations with North Korea?" Salon.com, February 3, 2002.

31. Nicholas D. Kristof, "North Korea's Secret," *New York Times*, January 16, 2003, p. 27.

32. Sigal, "North Korea Is No Iraq," p. 10.

33. Walter Pincus, "N. Korea Nuclear Plans No Secret," *Washington Post*, February 1, 2003, pp. 1, 6.

34. Sigal, "North Korea Is No Iraq," p. 11.

35. "U.S. Slams North Korea on Weapons," CBSNEWS.com, August 29, 2002.

36. "U.S. Rules Out Strike on North Korea," BBC News, World Edition, December 29, 2002.

37. Glenn Kessler, "Security Assurances Weighed for N. Korea," *Washington Post*, January 9, 2003, p. 1.

38. Walter Pincus and Glenn Kessler, "N. Korea Restarts Nuclear Facility," *Washington Post*, February 27, 2003, p. 23.

39. David Sanger, "U.S. Sees Quick Start to North Korean Nuclear Site," *New York Times*, March 1, 2003, pp. 1, 9.

40. Guy Dinmore and David Stern, "U.S. Issues Bleakest Warning Yet on N. Korea: Fears That Country May Sell Nuclear Material to Avoid Economic Collapse," *Financial Times*, February 5, 2003, p. 1.

41. Brent Scowcroft and Daniel Poneman, "Korea Can't Wait," *Washington Post*, February 16, 2003, p. B7.

42. Pincus and Kessler, "N. Korea Restarts Nuclear Facility," p. 23.

43. Sanger, "U.S. Sees Quick Start," p. 9.

Chapter 5. Ties That Bind?

1. Sabrina Tavernise, "Oil Prize, Past and Present, Ties Russia to Iraq," *New York Times*, October 17, 2002, p. A14.

2. Celeste A. Wallander, *Russia's Interest in Trading with the Axis of Evil*, policy memo no. 248, Program on New Approaches to Russian Security, Center for Strategic and International Studies, October 2002, p. 3.

3. Dimitri Trenin, *The End of Eurasia: Russia on the Border Between Geopolitics and Globalization*, Carnegie Endowment for International Peace, 2002, p. 166.

4. Grigory Yavlinsky, "The Iraqi War Will Not Spoil U.S.-Russian Ties," Radio Mayak (BBC Monitoring), March 29, 2003, pp. 1–2, at http://www.eng.yabloko.ru/Publ/2003/radio/radio_mayak_290303.html.

5. *The Times* (London), August 29, 2002, citing a Channel 4 documentary.

6. Karen DeYoung, "France Says It Is the Target of Untruths," *Washington Post*, May 15, 2003, pp. 1, 12.

7. Rubens A. Barbosa, "The United States After September 11 and the Effects on the World Order and Globalization: The Brazilian Position," paper presented to the National Forum, Rio de Janeiro, May 9, 2003, p. 5.

8. *Frontline*, "Blair's War," produced by Dai Richards, April 3, 2003, transcript p. 6.

Chapter 6. Opportunities Redux

1. Walter Pincus and Dana Priest, "Some Iraq Analysts Felt Pressure from Cheney's Visits," *Washington Post*, June 5, 2003, p. A1.

2. Nicholas D. Kristof, "Save Our Spooks," *New York Times*, May 30, 2003, p. 27.

3. Dana Priest and Walter Pincus, "Bush Certainty on Iraq's Arms Went Beyond Analysts' Views," *Washington Post*, June 7, 2003, pp. 1, 17.

4. Ibid.

5. Glenn Kessler, "Bush Sticks to the Broad Strokes," *Washington Post*, June 3, 2003, p. A01.

6. Glenn Kessler, "Bush Reacts Cautiously to Violence," *Washington Post*, June 12, 2003, p. A18.

7. Matthew Anthony Wier and John P. Holdren, *Controlling Nuclear Warheads and Materials: A Report Card and Action Plan*, Belfer Center for Science and International Affairs, Harvard University, March 2003, Executive Summary, p. xi.

8. Ibid., p. xv.

9. Howard Baker and Lloyd Cutler, Co-Chairs, *Report Card on the Department of Energy's Nonproliferation Program with Russia* (Washington, D.C.: U.S. Government Printing Office, 2001), pp. vi–vii.

10. Ibid., pp. iii–iv.

11. Wier and Holdren, *Controlling Nuclear Warheads*, p. xii.

12. John Newhouse, "The Threats America Faces," *World Policy Journal* 19, no. 2 (Summer 2002): 23.

13. Ibid., pp. 23–24.

14. Dan Stober, "Nuclear 'Bunker Busters' Sought," *San Jose Mercury News*, April 23, 2003, at http://www.bayarea.com/mld/mercurynews/news/5695904.htm.

15. Ibid.

16. Ian Hoffman, "Pentagon Wants New Nuclear Weapon, Defense Official Says," *Oakland Tribune*, April 8, 2003, at http://www.oaklandtribune.com/Stories/0,1413,82~1865~1310010,00.html.

Acknowledgments

I am grateful to Bruce Blair, the president of the Center for Defense Information, as well as my friend and colleague, for letting me write this book on CDI's premises. That helped a lot.

I am also indebted to my wife, Elizabeth Newhouse, for her support and also for the editorial "fixes" she provided. These improved the text.

Jenonne Walker agreed to read the manuscript, and in doing so offered a number of suggestions that made this a better book. I am indebted to her.

Lastly, I want to thank Ash Green, my editor on this and two other books, for his friendship and support.

Index

Index

186

Index

Index

Index

Index

Index

Peurifoy, Robert, 168
plutonium, 164
  of North Korea, 110, 112, 114,
    132, 135, 136
Poland, 147
Poneman, Daniel, 135
post–World War II era, 10–11, 149,
    155–6
Powell, Colin, 22–32, 145, 165
  as chairman of Joint Chiefs of Staff,
    11, 23
  G. W. Bush's speech as victory for,
    51–2
  Iraq policy and, 7, 23, 25, 29, 40,
    41–2, 45, 48, 51–7, 64–5, 66, 71,
    72, 147
  Korea policy and, 4, 24, 123, 124,
    127, 130–3
  loss of credibility by, 66
  Middle East policy and, 24, 26–31,
    52, 53, 161
  as multilateralist, 23, 55
  popularity of, 24, 25
  resignation option of, 25, 26, 28
  rolling over of, 24–6, 31
  Rumsfeld compared with, 23, 30–2,
    41
power, hard vs. soft, 151–2
preemptive force, doctrine of (G. W.
    Bush doctrine), 10–13, 21, 56,
    58, 66, 156
  non-American use of, 13, 48
  prevention and preeminence and,
    12–13
  regime change and, 12, 37
President's Foreign Intelligence
    Advisory Board, 47
Public Health Service, U.S., 20
Putin, Vladimir, 138–46, 169
  G. W. Bush's meetings with, 95,
    165
  G. W. Bush's relationship with, 10,
    36, 65, 99–102, 143–4, 149,
    150
  Iraq war and, 36, 43, 56, 64,
    149–50
  Yeltsin compared with, 98, 102,
    140, 142, 143
Pyongyang summit conference (June
    2000), 118

Quinlan, Sir Michael, 148

Rabin, Yitzhak, 40, 79
Ramallah, 28
Reagan, Ronald, 14, 17, 21, 29, 33
Reaganomics, 17
reconstitution capability, 166
refugees, 27, 108
regime change, 3–4, 6, 12, 13, 75
  in Iran, 81, 97
  in Iraq, 12, 13, 37, 38, 41, 42, 52,
    55, 57, 61, 73–4
  in North Korea, 157
religious zealotry, in U.S., 151
Republican Guards (Iraq), 39
Republican Party, 11, 14, 18–21
  arms control and, 33, 164, 167–8
  Congress controlled by, 16, 114
  Iraq war and, 36, 46–9, 60
  split on foreign policy in, 46
Reza Pahlavi, Mohammad, Shah of
    Iran, 78
Rice, Condoleezza, 22–3, 141
  China policy and, 105
  Korea policy and, 127, 133
Robust Nuclear Earth Penetrator,
    168–9
Rockefeller, Nelson, 32, 33, 34
Rogers, William, 24
rogue states, 7, 12, 129, 134–5
Roosevelt, Franklin D., 3, 17
Rove, Karl, 16, 17, 36, 156
Rudman, Warren B., 60–1
Rumsfeld, Donald, 9, 12, 22, 23,
    30–4, 145, 168
  China policy and, 105
  "Halloween Massacre" and, 32–3
  Iran policy and, 80–1
  Iraq war and, 36, 41, 47, 52, 57, 65,
    68, 69, 71, 75–6, 132
  Kissinger's conflict with, 32, 33
  Korea policy and, 127, 132
  Middle East policy and, 28, 31, 75
  near firing of, 31
  on old vs. new Europe, 65
  Powell compared with, 23, 30–2, 41
Rumyantsev, Alexander, 102
Russia, 51, 98–103, 138–46
  economy of, 100, 102–3, 139–40,
    141

Index

Index

Index

John Newhouse covered foreign policy for *The New Yorker* throughout the 1980s and early 1990s, and has written numerous profiles of world figures. He served the U.S. government as assistant director of the Arms Control Agency, and was senior policy advisor for European affairs in the State Department during the latter half of the Clinton administration. He is currently a senior fellow at the Center for Defense Information. He lives in Washington, D.C.

A NOTE ON THE TYPE

This book was set in Janson, a typeface long thought to have been made by the Dutchman Anton Janson, who was a practicing typefounder in Leipzig during the years 1668–1687. However, it has been conclusively demonstrated that these types are actually the work of Nicholas Kis (1650–1702), a Hungarian, who most probably learned his trade from the master Dutch typefounder Dirk Voskens. The type is an excellent example of the influential and sturdy Dutch types that prevailed in England up to the time William Caslon (1692–1766) developed his own incomparable designs from them.

Composed by Creative Graphics,
Allentown, Pennsylvania

Printed and bound by R. R. Donnelley & Sons,
Harrisonburg, Virginia

Designed by Virginia Tan